Mis·Inflation

Mis·Inflation

THE TRUTH ABOUT INFLATION, PRICING, AND THE CREATION OF WEALTH

DAVID L. BAHNSEN
& DOUGLAS WILSON

CANON PRESS

David L. Bahnsen and Douglas Wilson, *Mis-Inflation: The Truth about Inflation, Pricing, and the Creation of Wealth*
Copyright © 2022 by David L. Bahnsen and Douglas Wilson

Cover design by James Engerbretson
Interior design by Samuel Dickison and James Engerbretson

Printed in the United States of America.

All Scripture quotations are from the King James Version.

Library of Congress Cataloging-in-Publication Data forthcoming.

22 23 24 25 26 27 28 29 30 21   10 9 8 7 6 5 4 3 2 1

Contents

Preface

—WILSON

Part way through his life, Dante Alighieri found himself in a dark wood, and badly in need of a guide.

> Midway upon the journey of our life
> I found myself within a forest dark
> For the straightforward pathway had been lost.[1]

While not Dante's equal in anything aside from the lost-in-the-woods part, I have to say I have been fully his equal in having some questions that needed to be answered. Economics has been called a dark and dismal science for centuries, and resembled a dark

---

1. *The Divine Comedy*, trans. Henry Longfellow (London: George Routledge, 1867), *Inferno*, 1 [Canto 1, lines 1-3].

thicket closely enough to provoke me into asking some of my questions.

This was particularly the case when it came to those aspects of economics that I had thought I understood— like inflation, for instance. But I kept finding the actual events not seeming to confirm what I had been bracing for. In short, many of the predictions I had trusted somehow failed to materialize. And so a number of years ago I began to wonder, whatever happened to inflation? Specifically, it seemed to me that the government had been printing enough funny money to have us well into Weimar-levels of inflation by now, and so there I was, trying to figure out why it didn't seem to be happening. Now when you are in a dark and tangled wood like this, one naturally hopes to run into a Virgil of monetary policy, say, someone like David Bahnsen. And as much as I would love to extend this metaphor a bit more, I sense that our editors are getting restless and are thinking about staging an intervention.

I had been aware of David's work in the financial world for some years, and was really appreciative of his contributions to our public life together, particularly his book *Crisis of Responsibility*. One day it occurred to me that I could take this niggling question of mine about inflation, and just write to David and ask it. He was kind enough to reply, and that gave me the idea of writing a series of letters, thus getting a whole slew of questions answered, and for more folks than just myself. I then broached the idea of such a project with David, he was kind enough to agree, and you hold the results of that correspondence in your hands.

I thought it would be good to do this via written correspondence because the mistakes we conservatives make in economics really are tenacious mistakes. Because conservatives really do have a good grasp of most economic realities, it can be really hard for us to get our minds around the idea that we might not have everything dialed in. And so a written conversation enables us to go back and check the arguments when the old questions arise in our minds again—as they inevitably will. Let's say a couple years from now you go out and buy a gallon of milk for ten dollars. You might want to go back home again and pull this book down from the shelf for a little review and reassurance.

Please note. The question is not whether real inflation has happened in history, because we know that it has. The issue is whether that is the best explanation for what we see happening around us now. We are not arguing that the glass is half full when most conservatives say it is half empty. We are saying that everybody is looking at the wrong glass, and the one we are looking at is even emptier.

Not surprisingly, our discussion of inflation will touch on a number of other related issues. If you read these exchanges, you will come to understand the true definitions of inflation and deflation. You will come to learn why the apocalyptic-hyperinflation predictions have been wrong over and over again. You will see why commodity pricing (gas pump, groceries, etc.) is a bad benchmark for measuring inflation, and what a more reliable benchmark actually is. In these pages, we discuss how balanced budgets can be a good thing without them being the Holy Grail. We get into the sociological ramifications of gold-bug investing, and why your Uncle Wyatt really needs to think outside his safe box. We talk about how reckless government spending really is a catastrophic thing, but how the looming catastrophe might not be what everyone was anticipating—more like carbon monoxide poisoning than a giant fireball. You will learn why deflation is a lot less fun to think about, and why it is a much more likely scenario. And how do the government and the banks use and manipulate debt anyway? That's a good question too.

We conclude with a discussion of where true wealth resides, which is in the hearts, and minds, and families of entrepreneurs who are not risk-averse—because being risk-averse is tantamount to being love-averse. The government is guilty of regulatory suffocation when it comes to entrepreneurs, but it has to be said that some quarters of the conservative world are making their own contributions to that same kind of suffocation. We really need to find our way out of this dark wood.

In short, we have sought in these pages to provide an on-ramp for free-market conservatives who love the spirit of enterprise, and who want to put behind them a spirit of timidity and fearfulness.

Douglas Wilson
March 2022

Where Did the Inflation Go?

—WILSON

Dear David,

Knowing that fiscal policy is a passion of yours, and keeping in mind that it is an ongoing confusion of mine, I was wondering if I might trespass upon our friendship for a little bit. As I survey the decisions being made at the national and international level, I am having trouble fitting everything into a coherent picture.

I said that it was a confusion of mine, but it is a very particular kind of confusion. It is not the confusion of a cocker spaniel trying to understand quantum mechanics, which might be described as confusion across the board, on every level. This confusion of mine has to do with a body of knowledge that I have that I believe to be true, and trying to reconcile that with what is actually happening out there in the economy. All of it could be summed up in the question, "Where did the inflation go?"

If you decide to answer me, keep in mind that I am a layman in the realm of economics. But I am a layman who is generally well-read when it comes to economics "at the level of politics," you might say. This, to be distinguished from economics at the level of finance bankers, or hedge fund managers, or bitcoin junkies. My economic outlook would be an amalgam of Thomas Sowell, Friedrich Hayek, Milton Friedman, George Gilder, Frédéric Bastiat, Henry Hazlitt, Gary North, and so on. So put me down as a member of the old-timey inflation-is-theft/hard money school of thought.

My basic question (to start off with) is why the rapture hasn't happened yet. For my entire adult life, hard-headed fiscally responsible conservatives have been catching the last train out, and yet there always seems to be another train after the last train out. I believe that Gary North even wrote a book called *The Last Train Out*. And back in the eighties, Larry Burkett wrote *The Coming Economic Earthquake*, scaring the living daylights out of a lot of evangelicals.

So then conservatives are sitting on the roof, the morning after the rapture didn't happen, going over all the calculations yet again. The math still works.

Let me explain what I think inflation is, and you tell me why we aren't experiencing hyperinflation right now, given that the math still appears to work.

I have come to believe that inflation is to be understood as an increase in the currency supply chasing a non-increase in the number of available goods. So say that we had a very simple economy where one hundred dollars was available to buy one hundred widgets. What with one thing and another, the average cost of a widget would be one dollar. Now let us let loose a wicked Fed chairman, who releases another one hundred dollars into this very simple economy. If there is no corresponding increase in the number of widgets, then over time, as the adjustments shake out, the price of a widget will now be two dollars.

The scam aspect of this is that the first guy to show up with the new money is able to buy at the old prices, while the guy who shows up with the last new two dollars has to buy at the new price. This jiggering with the money supply creates an optical illusion for the man in the street, such that he thinks that prices are going up, when in fact that value of the currency is going down. He is not getting taller—the Fed has changed all the yardsticks, with the old half inches being now marked as inches.

Now this understanding of inflation seems to me to be reasonable, sane, logical, and a number of other good words. In addition, it budgets for *actual* price increases caused by other factors, and also allows for the radical price reductions that came out of a clearance sale for Pete's Furniture Warehouse. The average product, taking a broad average, is going to go up in price as a result of the devaluing of the currency.

Now given the amount of helium we have been pumping into the economy in recent years, it is a very real question to me why that economy hasn't floated off yet. By helium I mean the funds released through various "quantitative easings," the magic money of the pandemic stimulus checks, and all that.

So here is my question. Given what we have been doing to the currency, whatever happened to inflation? It seems to me that according to the classic fiscally conservative position, a loaf of bread should cost a hundred dollars by now.

None of this makes me want to jettison that classic understanding. I think it fully explains what happened to Germany in the Weimar Republic, or to Bolivia in the mid-eighties. What I don't get is why it isn't happening to us now.

It seems to me is that the answer has to lie in a number of complex variables, a bunch of which I have not yet imagined. But one of the possible candidates would be the fact of globalization—we are much more plugged into global markets than we used to be. To use a metaphor from one of my sons-in-law, peeing in the pool is still bad, but the pool is a lot bigger now.

Another variable (just shooting in the dark here) is that somebody somewhere is doing a countervailing "something" that turns out to be quite deflationary. For all the helium psi that is being pumped in the system, somebody is surreptitiously storing lead ingots in the basement. But apart from the weight of congressional ineptitude, I can't imagine what that might be.

Another possibility is that we are experiencing really bad inflation, but that the people responsible have figured out a way to "hide" it. A kind of "ledgerdemain."

So anyhow, there is my question. Given classical conservative economics, shouldn't we be experiencing radical inflation right now? Why aren't we? In your view, is the classic view wrong? Or are there variables in this new complex situation that we are not taking into account? Or something else?

Cordially in Christ,
Douglas

Fiscal vs Monetary Policy
—BAHNSEN

Dear Douglas,

Interestingly, there is a word choice in the very first sentence of your letter that I believe is going to prove important in my reply. You start off saying, "Knowing that *fiscal* policy is a passion of yours . . . ," while I am quite confident that you meant, "Knowing that *monetary* policy is a passion of yours." It would be pretty petty (and beneath me) if I were merely trying to nitpick or make hay of a minor vocabulary error, but in fact, I think that error will prove to be the very essence of where I believe our country stands as it pertains to the economic [in/de]flation debate.

Fiscal policy refers to that which impacts the economy from the "fiscal" side of the aisle—meaning, government policy. The low-hanging fruit here is usually tax policy (us supply-siders love fiscal policy when it means lowering the tax on growth and productivity), or else government spending (the Keynesian focus in fiscal policy for roughly seventy-five years).

But monetary policy refers to the actions of the central bank to effect their dual mandate—essentially, sound money and full employment. They are different tools, commanding differing schools of thought around each of them, and yet, many believe they are one and the same, *and these days, they are so dangerously entangled with one another,* people can be forgiven for conflating the two.

The question of, "Where did the inflation go?" is one that many are asking, and have been asking, for a long time. I hope that my answers here will help explain my point of view clearly and cogently, but more importantly, provoke a deeper understanding of the truly insidious decisions that have led us to the current state of affairs, one that I believe is quite concerning.

"Economics at the level of politics" is probably preferable to "economics at the level of a bitcoin junkie," but I digress. I assure you, most of the economic influences you cite were and are tremendous influences on me as well (Friedman, Gilder, Bastiat, Hazlitt). And I believe inflation as broadly understood is absolutely theft, and I believe most governments in history (including ours, now) would gladly take a higher inflation rate than we presently have as a means of inflating away much or most of their debt burden.

You cite some of the "doomsday" books other Christian economic influences on you have written. I want you to understand, I guess pastorally for me if nothing else, that the failed economic predictions of Christians essentially guided me into finance many years ago. While this biographical interlude may be irrelevant, in my case it gets to the heart of what I care about in a theology of wealth and finance.

If, and I do not believe this to *necessarily* be the case, but *if* we had to choose between (a) Christians who get the premises right and *the conclusions wrong*, OR (b) Wall Street or Ivy League dolts who get the premises wrong *but the conclusions right,* I could make a pretty good argument that when it comes to finance and investing, Option B is preferable. However, aside from the fact that Wall Street can get plenty of conclusions wrong too (whoever Wall Street is, but play along), the false dilemma of my set-up is that I don't believe Christians need to get the conclusions wrong. So I have made it my mission to find what premises in economics men and women of faith have, indeed, gotten right, and which they have gotten wrong. And from there, what is the reason we end up with such doomsdayism from most Christians in this space, divorced from empirical reality for decades?

I haven't figured it all out yet, but I have made a lot of progress. I hope that my life and work will prove to move the ball a bit towards the cause of economic cogency amongst men and women of faith, especially worldview-conscious ones.

So while I have my own sociological critiques of doomsdayism from "Christian economists," allow me to dive into the substance of your questions, especially as they pertain to inflation.

I essentially agree with your definition of inflation as "an increase in the currency supply chasing a non-increase in the number of available goods." I would add "and services" after "goods," and I would substitute "money" for "currency." But so far, so good.

But I think your example to reinforce your definition contains some flaws. We can pretend, since it is your example, that there are no new widgets in that simple economy, but to know if more money supply was needed to facilitate transaction of widgets we would have to know who held the money in circulation, what other goods and services besides that $1 widget came into being, and general employment and labor conditions. It is the very dynamic nature of a market economy that provide so many variables which impact money supply and the value of widgets. Supply and demand are not static, and neither are perceptions. "Humans act," von Mises taught us (though Solomon said the same thousands of years earlier). It is entirely possible that through other economic variables not in your equation circumstances changed in a simple economy where more money was needed to keep up with the goods and services of that economy.

But, and this is crucially important, what you describe *does happen,* and when it does, *it is a scam.* Now, if what we mean by that is that over time the prices a man pays for things have gone up 25%, *and his corresponding wages have not,* then we have a pretty clear moral outrage to call out. But if a man pays 25% more for goods and services over time, and also receives 25% more in wages, we may have *something* to call out, but it may not be the same moral outrage previously described.

This is one of the great reasons this conversation topic is so mightily improved upon when we focus on "quality of life" and "real returns"—that is, net of inflation—as opposed to price discussions. Price level talk becomes highly susceptible to the use of apples and oranges, whether disingenuously or accidentally. The classic example is the famous fifteen-cent-ice cream cone every grandfather talks about to his grandkids. Somehow, the real wages that era's businessmen earned never quite comes up in that tale! So

we have to do two things at once: Maintain the view
you have presented that inflation as a mechanism of a
deceiving scale or yardstick is wrong, and yet consider
that a more comprehensive measurement of transac-
tions is needed.

Your main question really advances to, "Why
hasn't all the increase of money pumped into the system generated inflation?" The "helium" you cite is
(a) stimulus checks, and (b) quantitative easing. And
prima facie, I am with you. But I will contend that neither stimulus checks or quantitative easing are actually "money pumping"—as much as our overlords
would like them to be.

Quantitative easing (QE) is a funky thing. It is not
money-printing, but it sure sounds like it is to most
people, and diving into technical and mechanical dif-
ferences does not do a lot to help bring clarity to the
conversation. Nevertheless, this clarity is important
for our purposes so I will try. No new cash or money
enters the economy as a result of QE (i.e. the definition
of money printing). Treasury bonds are pulled *out* of
the economy, and put on the balance sheet of the Federal Reserve. In this sense, it is an asset *swap*—not asset
creation. The Fed adds to bank reserves, and the banks
sell their treasuries to the Fed. The private sector does
not come out of the transaction with *more* money—
they come out of it with *different* money.

The banks do end up with massive excess reserves, and if the banks lent them all out, and consumers spent that borrowed money, it would result in a higher velocity of money, which combined with the increased money supply would perfectly meet the algebraic definition of more inflation.

But this leads me to the heart of the matter. Our government, fueled by a citizenry demanding it, has spent us into oblivion, which is to say, indebted us. Significant amounts of future growth have been pulled into the present, much like the family that buys a new big screen and patio set knowing next year's bonus will be able to pay it off. When that bonus comes, there is no growth—because it is paying off what was already bought with it. So we lose what we can't readily see—the growth we otherwise would have had. But in that example, the family at least got a TV and room full of furniture out of it. Eventually, what we spent the money on becomes less and less productive.

No expenditures carry less of a "multiplier effect" than government expenditures. So over time, the non-productivity of government spending actually contracts the economy, crowding out the private sector. We intuitively know this—private actors are better allocators of capital, or free enterprise wouldn't work and there wouldn't be such a thing as Hayek's "knowledge problem." Knowledge is, indeed, dispersed throughout the society in such a way that those with the most local knowledge of their local situation can most efficiently allocate capital and resources around that situation. Every dollar being allocated by a disinterested third party with a knowledge deficit is a dollar being sub-optimally allocated relative to the private actor with skin in the game, and with knowledge.

So we have a total economy that has grown rapidly (net of inflation), but with debt-to-GDP at higher levels, leading to lower expectations for growth into the future. Japan, the UK, and the EU are all in the same boat (none more so than the "thirty-year lacking in any inflation" nation of Japan). So when you imagine "who may be doing what" to facilitate disinflation or deflation, let me suggest a few culprits, two of which are benign, and two of which are horrific.

Yes, globalization is, on balance, a disinflationary force. I won't belabor this point. Now, I would argue we had a lot more globalization from 1991–2006 than we have from 2008–current, and the deflationary pressures have been more intense since the financial crisis than before it, but regardless, I accept globalization as a factor.

And the same is true of technology. The joke of the 1985 VCR for $800 is more significant than we understand. And while the iPhone may cost $1,000, we make a mockery of inflation analysis when we do not in some way account for a change in the utility of services that have price changes. The current iPhone has more computing power than every IBM mainframe at the Pentagon fifty years ago, *in one single iPhone*. To not have had disinflation one iPhone would have to cost $50 million. These are real and pertinent factors.

Demographics are a factor, too. Economic growth equals Population growth plus Productivity growth. Japan exacerbated their deflationary spiral by having a lot more old people dying than they had young people having babies. The U.S. kept a 2.1 fertility rate for quite a while, not enough for what I want to see, but better than Europe and godless Japan. We have gone down each year since the financial crisis, and both marriages and the 1.6 kids of child-rearing they produce, have been delayed from age twenty-three to age thirty-five. This is deflationary, and I should add, not good.

But there is no bigger factor behind low inflation levels in modern times than excessive government spending, the very thing many erroneously felt would be the cause of inflation. What they missed was what money is to begin with. How do we end up with new money in the economy? When the Fed prints it, and the bank has it, there has been no increase in circulation. *It is when the money is borrowed that it becomes new money* (and technically even then it has to be spent once it is borrowed). Loan demand has utterly collapsed in our country. Business investment is brutally low. Companies are already over-indebted so there is little borrowing capacity left to turn those excess reserves into new money. The ratio of loans-to-deposits in our banks is at the lowest it has been in fifty years, and with that decline in loan demand comes a collapse in velocity of money, the *sine qua non* of inflation.

I do not say this to celebrate the lack of inflation. I consider it a brutal financial outcome, but I also consider the suppression of growth from our economy that deflation represents totally unacceptable. We have not come close to achieving the 3.1% real GDP trendline growth we averaged for *decades* before the financial crisis, despite trillions of dollars of new deficit spending, additional national debt, and federal reserve machinations. We have a piper to pay.

The great economic achievement the doomsdayers missed out of the 1970s was the successful economic policy combination of marginal tax rate reductions unleashing a bonanza of productive output, as Paul Volcker was simultaneously stabilizing money with hawkish monetary policy (raising rates to kill inflation). The two things served not to just reverse the stagflation of the 1970s, but to create a totally underestimated era of real growth, real productivity, and real progress. Humans act, after all, and while government spending has never been on the responsibility train, that kind of output simply overwhelmed debt at the government level.

Add in the strong dollar policies of the Clinton years, the achievement of balanced budgets, and of course, great technological advancements, and voila—a great moderation of inflation had occurred.

Our challenges now have accelerated in the new century, primarily post-crisis. We have decided that our treatment for a patient who gets sick with too much debt (in the case of 2008, it was too much household debt) is more debt. We moved the debt from the balance sheets of households to the government, and now require a fiscal and monetary hair of the dog to prevent the hangover, in perpetuity. Low growth? Increase fiscal. Fiscal too expensive? Increase monetary. Monetary leads to a bubble that mis-prices risk and causes an asset liquidation? Treat it with more fiscal and more monetary.

Oh, and then COVID. Can you imagine where I am going with this?

With warm regards,
David

When Isn't a Stimulus Inflationary?

—WILSON

Dear David,

So I went and confused an Irishman for a Scot, didn't I? Got it—fiscal policy and monetary policy are two different animals. One barks and the other purrs. I understand everything now, and promise to try to be better.

In the past I have compared hard money economic analysts to men who have fallen off a skyscraper. Let's say that they have done so alongside some other people, and these others are somehow in denial. So on the way down, the hard money analysts have been seeking to persuade the ones in denial that we all, in fact, have fallen off that skyscraper. Their arguments are cogent, sound, and irrefutable. The fall has in fact happened. And then they ruin their ethos by saying something like, "and we are all going to hit the sidewalk in . . . *now*!" And then nothing happens because we are all still at the eighty-eighth floor. It seems to me that our team is really good at explaining the fact of having fallen off the skyscraper, and really bad at judging the distance to the sidewalk.

So your response was just the sort of thing I was hoping for, but while it beat back some of my questions, you successfully generated others. But before I get to those follow-up questions, let me see if I can summarize what you believe the two great hazards are. If I am reading you right, the things that concern you the most would be debt and deflation. In addition, I am assuming that later on in our exchanges you will explain to me how those two things are related—but that is merely a hopeful guess.

And on that matter of a debt crisis, I want to stick a pin in that because I suspect we will be talking more about that down the road. I have some questions about what a debt crisis might actually look like.

I am using the word *crisis* because you do use words like "horrific" and "quite concerning" and "insidious," while at the same time you are not wanting to encourage any kind of "doomsdayism." On this last point, is this because you don't believe there *could* be a catastrophic economic doomsday, or is it because you believe that no man can know the day or the hour? Is it because the fear is stupid and ungrounded, or is it because fear is a sin?

With all that out of the way, on to my new questions. I followed your explanation of QE perfectly. Not more money, but rather different money. But you also said that the stimulus checks weren't money pumping either, and that one has me stumped. I get how if the Fed just does a big swap with the banks, and the banks now have a bunch of liquid assets that they just sit on, not loaning most of it out, that would not be inflationary.

But why do the banks want to have all those assets without loaning the money out? What's the point? Are they just trying to make their books look good? Or are they trying to avoid inflating the currency? Inflation hurts the creditor, which the banks would then become, and creditors defend themselves against that by raising interest rates, which they can't do because of what that would do to the national debt, and why is this making my head hurt?

But back to the stimulus. The stimulus checks were mailed out to pretty much everybody, and in some cases, to their dog, and so then the American public ran out and bought up all the 9mm guns and ammo

they could find. How could that not be money-
pumping? All of it is now in circulation, right? The
money was created by fiat, and then mailed out to us
all, and then spent.

So let me modify my earlier definition of inflation
in accordance with your edits, and ask a follow-up
question, focusing just on the stimulus spending.
"Inflation is an increase in the money supply chasing
a non-increase in the number of available goods and
services." That being the case, when *would* stimulus
spending become inflationary? Would hyperinflation
set in if they sent every American a stimulus check for
a million dollars? Is there a tipping point?

You said this earlier: "But if a man pays 25% more
for goods and services over time, and also receives 25%
more in wages, we may have *something* to call out."
That makes sense to me, and so it seems to me that the
con is not being played on every consumer, but only
on a fraction of them. Isn't this part of the widget game
that is being played? In my first letter, I suggested that
the scam that was being run was that the first person to
show up with the new money gets to buy at all the old
prices, creating quite a deal for him. But the last person to get the new money has to go out and buy at the
new prices. This doesn't hurt him any—as you point
out, he spends 25% more on goods and services, but he
also has 25% more money. All we have done for *him* is

move the decimal point. Thus it seems that the profit being raked off in the scam is somewhere in the transition point, the sweet spot where some lucky fellow has a bag of new money and a world full of old prices. Or am I missing something there?

But I come back to the troubling fact that there seems to be a lot of new money, and not a lot of inflation. The fact that classic inflation does not appear to have happened makes me want to troubleshoot the possible options, which present themselves to me as follows:

The definition of inflation above is wrong. Inflation is caused by something else;

The inflationary pressures are there, just as described, but there are countervailing deflationary pressures (e.g. globalization), causing everything to equal out somehow;

Inflation is in fact occurring, but it is being cleverly masked by trickery and lies. The prices of certain markers or staples are kept artificially low, while the prices of other goods and services are allowed to go through the roof.

We need to look at percentages of new money, not amounts of new money. Maybe the economy has gotten a lot bigger, and so looking at the amount of new money doesn't tell us anything because we need to look at the ratios.

Some combination of the above . . .

Or I left out the most obvious explanation for some reason, and have done so in a way as to invite you to set me straight.

I do have other related questions, which I trust we will get to, but I am struggling manfully to not put them all in one letter.

> Cordially in Christ,
> Douglas

The Benchmark of Inflation

—BAHNSEN

Dear Douglas,

The second batch of questions are perfectly logical follow-ons to the first batch, and I hope the second batch of answers moves us in a good direction. All of these things are complicated but it seems to me we are making progress, both in laying out a few definitions and then trying to unpack how one thing (properly defined) leads to another.

I do think the skyscraper analogy you use helps with one aspect of the hard money analyst errors—their use of flawed timing to accompany their predictions. But I

would add two things to the mix that may or may not
be agreeable to you:

1. I do not believe *all* hard money (and certainly not
    all *sound* money) advocates work off of the "we
    have fallen off a skyscraper" mentality. Some are
    more extreme in their doom and gloom than
    others, to say the least. Upon further inquiry,
    one cannot help but notice that oftentimes the
    true "we have fallen off a skyscraper" folks have
    a business model that benefits from more wild
    rhetoric, one way or another. But of course ben-
    efiting from a prediction does not make the pre-
    diction inherently false, but it may help explain
    the desire to attach a timeline to the fall.

2. The other piece I would suggest is that it seems
    to me hard money advocates are not merely say-
    ing "we have fallen off a skyscraper, and here's
    when we crash." They have stated *why* we have
    fallen off the skyscraper, which way we will blow
    on the way down, and what the crash will be like.
    They have provided ample levels of specificity,
    and not merely been wrong about the timing, but
    multiple cause and effect periphery as well.

I believe it is entirely appropriate for a sound money
advocate (of which I am one, but you will note I find

the adjective *sound* money preferable to *hard* money, for a variety of reasons) to believe "we have an economic milieu right now that is going to prove problematic." But falling off a skyscraper means death, it means a violent death, and it means a pretty sudden death. And judging by those three criteria, the economic doom and gloom camp not only has been wrong, but cannot possibly know that they one day will be right. In other words, I would not grant that they "have gotten it all right but the arrival date." This is a big bone of contention for me in the field of economics, and generally it is with left-wing economics—hubris belongs on the basketball court, not in a field where you are dealing with trillions of variables of unknowns. I particularly desire this added component (humility) with Christian economists.

But back to some of the points you make in your most recent response . . . I really don't want to be a stickler about semantics in each and every correspondence (life is too short), and my first letter issue about fiscal vs. monetary was only important because I consider it so substantive. But I would add from the most recent letter that "the things that concern me most right now being debt and deflation" is essentially correct, with one thing being created by the other. In other words, my contention is that the lesson of history is that excessive debt creates deflationary pressures. So I only worry about deflation because of the debt, which is another way of saying—I worry about the debt and all the insidious things it represents. I actually don't even worry about the debt as much as I worry about the size of the government. I like to put it this way when I have talked to other like-minded conservatives.

> Scenario #1: A government where its spending is 15% of GDP, and it runs a budget deficit that is 2.5% of GDP.

> Scenario #2: A government where its spending is 25% of GDP, and it runs a perfectly balanced budget.

Where the budget deficit is lower than the nominal rate of growth in the economy, and where the portion of the economy the government represents is smaller, not greater, is far preferable to me than no budget deficit and a massive, growing, large government presence in the economy. Now, I am all for someone saying, "I want smaller government *and* a balanced budget," and that sounds like a great ideal to me, too. But pro-growth, supply-side tax cuts in the Jack Kemp/Art Laffer/George Gilder/Ronald Reagan world resulted in budget deficits that shrank as a percentage of the economy, even though they were deficit-funded. I think some conversation about the "ideal" is useful, but for our purposes, I simply want to point out (because I believe it is really important to this conversation) that in the binary choice between a larger government with no debt and a smaller government with debt, I take the debt.

But that is because what I am ultimately after is not merely a clean balance sheet, but a right-sized citizenry. Self-government can exist in scenario #1 and I do not believe it can exist in scenario #2. Besides the fact that any government growing its size relative to the overall economy, will, eventually become indebted, too, the fact of the matter is that balancing one's budget with an egregious tax code and regulatory burden is the opposite of what we want, no matter how it looks on the P&L. There is only one sustainable way to get the growth we want in an economy, and ultimately avoid the inflationary and deflationary parasites that come with various government abuses—and that is a smaller government as a percentage of GDP. If we focused on that—the disease—rather than the various other peripherals, we'd be contributing more cogent thought to the policy needs of the moment.

So excessive debt *as indicative of excessive size of government* is my top concern, and yes, I am convinced it is ultimately deflationary in an advanced economy that possesses the world's reserve currency.

Your next paragraph is really useful in giving me a chance to reinforce something I said a few paragraphs ago. Your question was:

> I am using the word crisis because you do use words like "horrific" and "quite concerning" and "insidious," while at the same time you are not wanting to encourage any kind of "doomsday-ism." On this last point, is this because you don't believe there could be a catastrophic economic doomsday, or is it because you believe that no man can know the day or the hour? Is it because the fear is stupid and ungrounded, or is it because fear is a sin?

I believe that when one sees risk in policy error but does not know how those risks will play out, it behooves them to lay low on the melodrama. I guess it is fair for me to add, "especially when one's melodrama has been wrong for fifty years or so." But this gets back to that point of humility in economics—I am all for calling out bad policy, and intelligently deciphering the various potential outcomes of such, but my business model does not require doomsdayism, and so more constrained (and humble) adjectives seem more appropriate to me.

And yes, I do believe despair is a sin. If I did have a crystal ball of some *particular* economic catastrophe with *particular* timing, I'd still prefer to avoid despair. Solutions, not fear. Life is too short to be ruled by fear, unless your revenue model is a paid newsletter. (Okay, now I am just being snarky.)

Let's unpack your questions about bank reserves and QE, etc. You end up asking a question that I actually think really tees up the heart of the matter.

You refer to the banks having "assets" without loaning the money out. What the Fed has on their balance sheet are "assets" (the Treasury bonds and mortgage bonds they have purchased), and what banks have is the cash that the Fed has credited to them for the purchase of those assets. Yes, the Fed credits that cash with money that does not exist (i.e. money printing, of a sort). The Treasury has to pay back the money they borrowed, and the Fed is the recipient of that cash when it happens. If the Fed were to cancel that debt it would be overt monetization of the debt, but that would be both illegal and improbable, which is to say, we'll keep watch. But I digress . . .

You ask why banks would want that money without loaning it out, and in this question we get to the heart of the matter. *Banks make money when they lend it out. That is what the business of banking is—the collection of a spread in money earned vs. money paid on deposit.* And banks don't need to make their books look good—regulatory requirements do that for them! By definition, this represents "excess reserve requirements"—above and beyond Fed regulatory stipulations. Now, I don't want to get *too* into the weeds here, but there is no question that maintaining liquidity surpluses benefits banks in the post-crisis era. There is a push–pull for banks to find optimal equilibrium between liquidity needs and the opportunity cost of keeping these excess reserves. There is no question that banks prefer some excess reserves for both emergency liquidity needs, margin of error on the regulatory front, and the opportunity that may come up for a future spending/lending situation vs. the last one they just funded. However, there is simply no greater reason for the level of excess bank reserves than the *complete deflationary collapse of loan demand.*

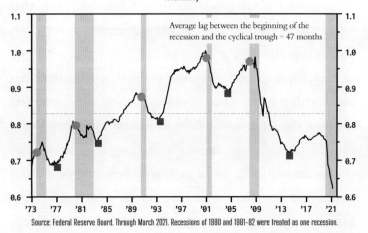

Total Loan to Deposit Ratio:
All U.S. Commercial Banks (1973–2021)
monthly

Average lag between the beginning of the recession and the cyclical trough = 47 months

Source: Federal Reserve Board. Through March 2021. Recessions of 1980 and 1981-82 were treated as one recession.

The Fed has made holding reserves marginally more attractive by paying interest on these reserves (currently a mere 0.10%). If the Fed wanted to *charge* for excess reserves, they could do so. That would likely result in a very different environment. But it would not and could not create loan demand; it would only create bad loans, bad underwriting, bad incentives, and a really bad final outcome.

So the Fed has short term treasury rates at record lows, which makes the opportunity cost of holding cash vs. Treasury bills a big donut. Excess reserves do not make the banks money, but they are not costing the banks money (in opportunity cost). That, combined with the *deflationary reasons for collapsing loan demand*, has made the holding of exorbitant excess reserves the "least bad option" for banks.

I think the better question is not, "Why do the banks want this?" but rather, "Why does the Fed want this?" Essentially, the Fed is in the midst of this negative feedback loop, what I am calling a deflationary spiral, where their interventions to the business cycle (through hyper-accommodation) has created more dependency in the business cycle on the tools they have used, so that more of the same is required to get yet more of a diminished return for their efforts. My last note spoke of the diminished return of *fiscal* stimulus (through time, you get a negative multiplier on Keynesian demand-side spending). But there is no question that the same principle applies to *monetary* stimulus as well. On the margin, dropping rates from 4% to 1% is pretty impactful; dropping from 1% to 0% is less so.

And this also speaks to the collapsing loan demand. As past monetary stimulus worked its way through, borrowers naturally responded to incentives. Large corporations, for example, that saw a 10% return on certain projects now became willing to borrow at a 2–3% cost of capital. Fair enough. But at some point, the high quality borrowers hit a wall. They lever up to the highest point they can (which may or may not be higher than the highest point they should), and that means one thing *for the future: There is no one left to borrow (without really hurting the credit quality of the borrowing).*

NFC Debt Burden

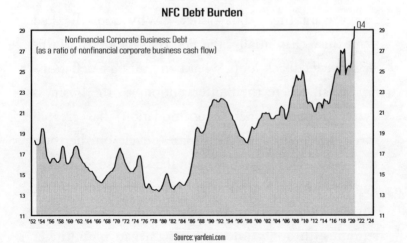

Source: yardeni.com

So now you have too much borrowing in the system (that initially can become stimulative as good borrowers invest in good projects at high returns and low cost of capital), which leads to less new loan demand, despite attractive rates at which to borrow. The Fed cannot create *projects to invest in,* and it cannot create *quality borrowers.* It can only create the paper money to put on shelves, and a low cost to pay for borrowing it. The process is now pushing on a string. See: Japan.

And this gets down to the inflation thesis. Hopefully I have well-explained why loan demand has dropped and why QE/bank reserves cannot help that dilemma. But what this whole process does is collapse the velocity of money, which is the *sine qua non* of inflation (the turnover of money in the society).

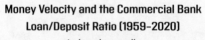

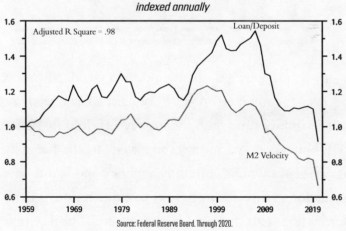

Money Velocity and the Commercial Bank Loan/Deposit Ratio (1959-2020)

indexed annually

Source: Federal Reserve Board. Through 2020.

Moving on to your next point—the stimulus checks were real circulated money. Now this is undeniable, sort of. The stimulus checks went from the government to the bank accounts of the people receiving them. And a bunch of that money was spent. You see some of that reflation in the data now. But a whole bunch of it was not spent. It was received, and saved.

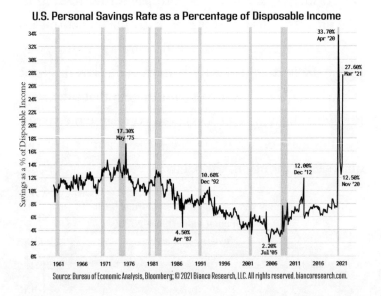

U.S. Personal Savings Rate as a Percentage of Disposable Income

Or it was received, spent, and then saved. Meaning, a lower-income person got it, bought a flat screen and a new iPhone, and then the money sits. Johnny makes $15/hour, got free money, and went to the bar with it. The bar owner got Johnny's money and had to save some for a rainy day or pay off past due rent to a landlord who is past due on a mortgage, etc. This is where that collapsed velocity comes from out of excessive debt—future growth and spending was pulled into the present by past borrowings, and the society can't get past this deflationary spiral.

I should add, the pitifully low savings rate of Americans is why we have the trade deficits with other countries we have, and it is also why, in periods of excess cash infusions, velocity stays low and bank accounts go higher. We are always playing catch-up with the right thing to do.

You ask if the government could send $1 million to every man, woman, and child and that would remain non-inflationary (i.e., where is the tipping point?). But the government can only send what it has, and it can only have what it earns in tax revenue, *or else borrows*. Its transfer payment largesse is limited by its borrowing capacity (that is actually a painful sentence to type, since neither its largesse or its borrowing capacity seem all that limited, I grant you). But yes, they are limited by some number, and that number is the interest rate at which it can be funded. Now, if the Fed wanted to monetize all of this, we could get a really market-distortive, inflationary pile of garbage, and all bets are off. But the fact of the matter is that the Fed owns only about 20% of the national debt, and the U.S.'s relative ranking in global economic strength, its appeal to foreign investors, and status as the world's reserve currency, have allowed it to finance its spending without an explosion of rates. What would make rates go higher?

Higher inflation expectations.

The bond market is the judge and jury here.

Moving on to your point about the unequal impact of increases in the price of goods and services relative to the increase of wages—if I understand what you are getting at here, I am in complete and total agreement. That policy decision is not, and cannot be, evenly distributed in the society. I absolutely believe that the present policy paradigm is more beneficial to those who hold assets (real estate and stocks, for example) than those who do not. And a year-by-year increase in prices (modest as it has been) hurts those who are more sensitive to such expenditures than those who are not. I am in full agreement with you—"mild" inflation is more unfair to lower income people than higher income people, and asset price inflation is more beneficial to those who hold assets than those who do not. I believe both of these conditions exist, and both of these conditions are wrong. They are reasonably fixable by policy, though not without a trade-off. The Fed has determined that trade-off is not worth it.

In the end, when we look at your potential explanations for why there appears to be a lot of new money but not a lot of inflation, I would say that:

Inflation's definition is not the problem—it truly is too much money chasing too few goods and services. A growing economy needs more money in the money supply because it has more goods and services absorbing such.

You are correct that, absent various deflationary countervailing pressures, there would be more inflation. I simply believe that the most prominent of deflationary pressures (along with globalization, technology, and demographics) is excessive debt.

I do not believe we can plausibly argue that "inflation is being masked by trickery and lies." Where there is inflation, it is not covered up very well (housing, higher education, health care—the trinity of evil price inflation). Ultimately, the judge and jury I referred to earlier is the key ingredient here—the bond market. TRILLIONS of SMART dollars cannot buy ten-year government paper at 1.5% if they believe that it will be subject to 4%, 6%, or 8% annual inflation between now and then. If financial actors were all that stupid, we got capitalism wrong.

Yes, indeed, new money needs to be looked at relative to the overall size of the economy (the size of the goods and services). But this is a tautology.

I think we are left with nothing but the Occam's razor, which is that reckless government spending and the desire to "smooth" the business cycle with fiscal and monetary interventions have created a Japan-like deflationary environment, for now. Central bankers believe they can fix inflation (we had it once, and we fixed it). They do not believe they can fix deflation (the PTSD of the depression rightfully lives on). And all policy stems out of those conditions or beliefs.

I alluded a moment ago to inflation in health care, housing, and higher education. I believe these three things—generationally and empirically undeniable— are all three created by bad policy, but not predominantly by monetary inflation. I so often fear that my stance on these issues we are discussing will be misconstrued by like-minded friends and allies that I offer these points as a basic summary of my position:

One can reject the hyperinflation or high-inflation thesis while still believing that 2% annual inflation is reckless and wrong.

One can believe that purposeful inflation is theft (it is) while still believing that the avoidance of any inflation (or deflation) is easier said than done.

The truly impactful examples of price inflation in the last forty years have been in housing, health care, and higher education, and in all three cases it was governmental policies—not central banking ones—that are the insidious and guilty culprit. I can elaborate on all this for days, and did to some degree in my first book.

Because there is no such thing as an aggregate price level, it is important to establish a benchmark for measuring inflation. My contention is that the bond market has been so forever, and will continue to be so.

I am not a fatalist about how this ends, but nor am I sanguine. I believe it is entirely possible the end-run will be decades of slow/low/no growth—Japanification. It isn't sexy to deny the doomsdayers a "big bang" moment. I've noticed that many who don't believe in a dramatic Armageddon-like end to history sort of need to believe in one in the middle of history. I can't say there won't be such a skyscraper-fall splat, but I can say that being stuck in an elevator in an skyscraper for thirty years doesn't sound much better, even if it makes for a less exciting movie.

I look forward to the future dialogue, especially where it may be necessary for me to be more clear than I have been. For any failures of clarity, I apologize in advance.

With warm regards,
David

What Makes Deflation Bad?

—WILSON

Dear David,

Thanks very much. This is actually getting at my basic questions, at least the ones that started all this. But, not to be tedious, it also leads (of necessity, I think) to a few additional questions.

Your modifications to my skyscraper analogy are entirely acceptable to me. It was my disquiet over so many predictions not coming to pass that led me to want to pursue this subject with you in the first place. Although, speaking of that, I do want to ask about something else in passing. In recent weeks, I have seen a number of people pointing at phenomena that they say

are the harbinger of the coming Biden inflation tsuna-
mi—the price of gas, price of eggs, prices of lumber, etc.
If I am understanding you properly, you would say that
the indicator of *actual* inflation, were it to happen, would
be the bond market, and that these other things would
be localized fluctuations, driven by various factors, stupid government decisions among them (e.g. lockdowns).
Is that it? And besides, I don't want to be guilty of a bait
and switch discussion, beginning by asking why there
isn't any inflation, listening carefully to your answer, and
then asking how you account for all the inflation then.

So your response on what the stimulus money is
doing (and/or not doing) made really good sense to me.
People are being fairly responsible with the irresponsible handouts, thus making the handouts less irresponsible, at least with regard to possible inflationary
impact. The stimulus does add to the debt load, and
hence to the long term deflationary pressures, but it
has not resulted in a short term inflationary burst. Do I
understand you correctly? This is because they basically gave everybody a bottle of whiskey to go get liquored
up in order that they might spend a lot of money, but
then instead of that everybody put their whiskey in the
cabinet to be brought out for toasts on anniversaries
and other special occasions.

In addition, you and I are in complete agreement on
the debt amounts v. debt ratios thing. It doesn't help us

to be told that the federal debt is $bazillion unless we are willing to ask, "Compared to what?" If the government debt load is shrinking relative to the GDP, then we are moving in a direction where government spending has decreasing influence over a growing economy. This seems to me to just be common sense, and highly to be desired—compared to what we are doing now. Would I rather live under a gargantuan government ruled over by fiscally responsible despots, who balanced the budget (on our backs) every year, or a government that was running a budget deficit for a little putt-putt bureaucracy. You and I would make the same choice.

So then. The thing to be bracing for is debt-driven *deflation*, which leads me to two sets of questions.

The first has to do with two different kinds of debt, and what kind of debt creates the deflationary pressure— unless they both do. The first kind of debt would seem to be one that creates the potential for true loss, or a real opportunity cost, straight up. Say that someone borrows 50K from a friend to start up a business, but he winds up spending it on beer and cocaine instead. The investor is simply out, and has to write it off as a bad debt—but what he is writing off is real money that he used to have. This money that he used to possess is money that he could have invested elsewhere, but now he cannot.

But it seems to me that there is another kind of debt. Suppose that two friends are watching a football game, and drinking too much also, and while in their cups, they bet each other a million dollars on the outcome of the game, money that neither one of them actually has. One of them loses the bet, naturally, and the two of them have words the next day. This was "money" that was created by the beer, and it can't actually go away because it was actually never there. There could be possible real world consequences beyond hard feelings if the winning friend had gone out and bought a car he couldn't afford on the strength of winning the bet, but for the most part this seems like indebtedness without any real money involved.

Now it seems to me—and I am counting on you to set me straight here—that our government plays with both kinds of debt. When they borrow real money to pay researchers to study why snails have two antennae, they are precluding productive inventors and entrepreneurs from being able to borrow that money. The government squandering money like this creates opportunity costs. This is not to say that the money spent on snail research is simply incinerated, but the money is not allocated as intelligently as it would have been had it been invested in response to market information. The money is still in the economy, just as the money spent on beer and cocaine is still in the economy, but it could have done a lot more good elsewhere. So government debt of this sort is the kind that wastes a genuine resource.

So when they promise us all our entitlements (Social Security, health care, etc.) decades into the future, what we like to call "unfunded liabilities," this seems more like the two guys betting on the football game. Only a twenty-five-year-old fool would go buy a new car on the basis of an outlandish drunken bet, and only a twenty-five-year-old fool would refuse to prepare for retirement because "he had Social Security."

Would you distinguish the two kinds of debt in this way? And if not, what sort of names could you call me to get me to see things more clearly? And why does debt create deflationary pressure?

The second big question concerns what deflation actually looks like, and how thoughtful Christians should be preparing themselves. I think that a lot of us understand what would happen in the course of runaway inflation, meaning that we have some idea what it would look like. But what does *deflation* look like? What happens actually? Is it simple stagnation? Or is there a crash involved? You have used the example of Japan a few times. Is that it? Or is Japan merely on the cusp of the impending deflation?

Are inflation and deflation just two different ways of crashing the airplane, one into a mountainside and the other into a lake?

If I might, could I use an illustration that might be pertinent to some of the people who might read a book

like this? This is not to praise (or throw shade on) those
who have been buying gold for years now, and who
have it safely buried in a box behind the barn. Rather,
I am just trying to get my mind around what deflation
actually is, and I would like to hold the definition up
against a gold coin.

So suppose a guy has a shoebox full of American
Eagles, and inflation radically reduces the value of the
paper currency—because currency is what the government can print, and which they industriously do. But
they can't print Eagles, and so the gold maintains (more
or less) the same purchasing power it had before the runaway inflation. The value of the currency is going down
relative to the gold, which is why it now takes a thousand dollars to buy a loaf of bread. Thus far inflation.

But what happens to this guy and his gold in a time
of deflation? Did he do exactly the wrong thing? Or is
he protected now as well, only just not for the reasons
he thought he was going to need protection?

I hope that this last question makes sense. I think it
boils down to, "What makes deflation bad?"

Cordially in Christ,
Douglas

Wealth Creation

—BAHNSEN

Dear Douglas,

I believe the answer to your question is essentially a very clean "yes"—that the bond market is the judge and jury on inflation, and that there can be a plethora of other circumstances when we look at various price fluctuations. I will elaborate a bit in the present context, but if one sentence were needed to summarize then, yes, bond yields tell us more about inflation than potentially idiosyncratic price movements.

But let's unpack that further. Copper prices were $2.25 as COVID lockdowns and uncertainty began. They are $4.34 now, though that is down nearly 10%

from where it was just two months ago. Regardless, prima facie, this appears to be a 100% inflation in copper prices from that COVID moment. Now, even those who fear sustainable inflation acknowledge that "base effect" realities make this pretty disingenuous—that measuring the price movement from a particular low level created by exogenous circumstances skews reality. So we can look to the pre-COVID period of 2019 and see copper of roughly $3—well higher than its collapse to $2.25, but still way lower than its current price above $4. So case closed, right? A crucial industrial metal like copper points to significant price inflation even when measured outside of COVID circumstances . . .

But there is a problem! Copper was $4.54 in 2011. Over a perfect ten-year calendar period we have had . . . 0% price movement in the most significant industrial metal in American life. And I think this is the danger in measuring inflation around a given commodity price. First, the start and end points can be quite selective and matter a lot. Second, the price experience for given commodities will be highly different from other commodities based on non-monetary realities (oil's supply/demand crux, not to mention OPEC cartel factors, have different drivers than say, corn). And finally, as people look at 2021 price movements to validate an inflation thesis they will be disappointed to pull the timeline back further, where an actual structural and secular trend can be more demonstrated . . . for in nearly all cases, one- or two-year price inflation looks like absolute disinflation when we move further back. And if prices are flat over ten years, that simply is not inflation.

In other words, the bond market got it right all along, as it always does.

The short-term idiosyncratic things that may very well speak to 2021 price movements are heightened right now for a lot of reasons. Supply-chain disruptions are at the top of that list. Supply-chain disruptions push prices higher. And supply-chain disruptions in this case are nearly all the fault of thoughtless government interventions (or market responses to government overreach). This is an important theme in our correspondence: ***Nowhere am I absolving the government of their share of the blame in these things; I am simply pointing to different causes and effects than I think my friends on the right and in the Church have often been programmed to point.***

Government incompetence goes deeper and wider in my worldview than I think it does in many of my friends' worldviews, if that makes sense.

I will add to the whiskey analogy below as it pertains to *structural inflation*—I do think it is true that the government gave a lot of people whiskey in hopes of them getting liquored up, and a lot of people stored it for future entertaining. But I think where the analogy is perhaps a little incomplete is in this pivotal economic tautology . . . *When it comes to getting inflation, another major obstacle is not that people just keep doing this gosh-darn responsible thing, but that there is not room for more imbibing—meaning, the real loan demand needed to create inflation has to come from companies, and companies are already levered up from the last round of low rates and spending.*

To twist on the whiskey analogy, you can hope the bottle you bought the drunk results in him drinking even more, but that is really hard to do when he is already passed out. (I think we've taken this one as far as it will go.)

Now, even my add-on analogy fails here because I am not saying anything negative about the company that has levered up and no longer needs to add leverage, whereas the drunk who drinks no more because he is facedown in the gutter does denote a pretty negative image. But my point is that there is a diminishing return that is at the heart of the economic lesson I am preaching. Productive use of debt exists, and many companies have used such over the years. Then maybe a little more. But as debt-to-income and debt-to-asset ratios get stretched, the amount of productive projects to put capital into decreases and the capacity for more debt servicing decreases, *no matter how much whiskey the Fed gives the company.*

Okay, now I really am done with the analogy.

Your analogy of the two kinds of debt is fascinating, because it actually does help reinforce what is the heart of the matter here, whether you did so intentionally or not. I would argue that the first example you offer of "real money" debt between friends is dangerous (capital gets destroyed), and the second one is not (because no one is ever going to pay that debt; there is no capital lost because friend A is not going to pay it and friend B did not go spend his real capital believing friend A would pay; these two parties have the option of "liquidating" the debt—acknowledging insolvency—avoiding the chain reaction of debt deflation).

But to your point, our government participates in *both* kinds of debt, *yet in the government's case, the second category automatically becomes the first category, because* **real capital** *gets spent when "funny money" is promised, circulated, and extended.* The option of "liquidating" the debt does not exist (for all practical purposes). So the second category with the government is really one and the same with the first—capital is extended; capital is lost; wealth is reduced. So the deflationary pressure in the second category of funny money debt (when the government is the borrower) is that real debt exists on the balance sheet, and it will get paid back (and serviced along the way), reducing GDP capacity for productive investment.

The algebraic reality is that National Savings is always and forever reduced by Government Spending. Investment can ONLY come from savings (there is no dollar invested, ever, that is not first saved). In a nationally aggregated sense, less dollars are saved by more dollars being government-spent. Therefore, there is an inverse correlation between government spending and national investment. Now, this cannot be controversial because it is all math. But in my final conclusion, that reduced investment means compressed potential for growth and productivity (the deflationary pressures of which I speak), one doesn't have math to appeal to for agreeing or disagreeing with the statement; they may just want to assert that, no, greater investment does not help productivity. They may want to assert that reduced investment is good for growth. At that point, I wouldn't argue with their math but I would argue with their wisdom.

Your final question about what deflation looks like is very difficult to answer. I am so critical of economists who claim to know certain unknowable things that I want to walk on eggshells to avoid doing the same. My best thesis is what I call "Japanification," and it is primarily evidenced in long-term periods of economic stagnation. Japan had a bubble burst (the 1990s), and then a period of long term deflation. They are just now coming out of it, but can't really get *out of it* (260% debt to GDP, now). They simply haven't grown, flourished, or innovated in a generation. And yes, there was a "crash" when the bubble burst—asset prices were re-priced from very high, to much lower.

If I could offer a slight criticism of the reconstructionist view on these things, it is what I imagine to be their own "visualization" of these things (and maybe I am just projecting here). I believe many well-meaning believers were programmed to believe in a "bang" moment, when perhaps this all ends with a whimper. T.S. Eliot had something to say here.

My own view is that the practical steps one ought to take to protect against the economic risk and damage done by a society that lives above its means far transcends things like a shoebox of gold coins. One could say, "Inflation didn't come the way we thought it would, but my gold has maintained its purchasing power," but they would be wrong. Gold is currently 30% below its inflation-adjusted price of the late 1970s. For an entire generation gold has failed to do what it was promised to do—as its sole and inherent function in the universe!

But of course, many people also bought homes, stocks, and bonds, and therefore had assets that did appreciate even as their gold (in real terms) did not. I am not being critical of an investment decision; I am more speaking to a mentality.

I believe the practical applications of this dialogue are vast. But none is more important to me than re-starting the process of Christian testimony on economics and policy in the public square. I believe the one-note inflation issue has compromised that, and made right-wing believers too synonymous with survivalists and inflation hawks, unable to meaningfully contribute to the conversation about why government spending is suffocating economic growth. Ironically, Pastor, those who believe the government will create inflation from their ill-conceived policies are *validating* the government policy (back to an earlier point—the government most certainly *wants* to create inflation; my argument is that they're not very good at it).

I suppose my agenda may be more specific in the focus of my calling and career (providing truth and application around economic challenges) and yours may be more specifically pastoral given your calling and career. But I think how thoughtful Christians prepare for the current economic realities touches both of our callings. Whether I was approaching it with the wisdom of a financial professional trying to prepare an investor-client to successfully meet an objective, or a pastor trying to protect a flock from economic malaise, I believe the best solutions to defending against inflation and deflation are found in enterprise.

Wealth creation is not merely an Adam Smith or classical economic construction. It is entirely anthropological, and it transcends the unfortunate inflationary and deflationary impact of government intrusions (all of which—every single one—are urged on by the population). Therefore, I believe the best defense against stagnation, price distortions, and all sorts of economic malady, is the wealth creation of human action. This makes me a very equity-oriented guy. It's not "the stock market"—it's the miracle of wealth creation from the actions that create growth. Self-interest. Stewardship. Creation mandate. Incentives. All these things. And yes, it could be publicly traded equities that scratch these itches, but it also could be one's own business, or a fund of ten privately run businesses. The details are probably outside our scope, but the underlying theme is not.

Believing in a pending big bang economic earthquake and thinking gold will somehow help in such a case is a sociological construction.

Believing in and acting on the realities of enterprise and markets as a condition for human flourishing is a theological construction.

I pick B.

With warm regards,
David

How Can the Government Handle Debt?

—WILSON

Dear David,

Thank you very much for all of this. It is most helpful, extremely clarifying, and maybe even a little diverting.

So let me summarize what I think I have learned from you. Please let me know if I am taking this in any direction you think unhelpful, or which misconstrues you in any way. And then after that summary, I do have a few more questions.

So the specter that is haunting us is the burden of debt, unpayable debt, and ever-increasing debt. As this debt accumulates, the servicing of the debt has various ways of eating up money that could have been used for productive investments. The outcome of that unfortunate circumstance is that economic growth is hindered or stifled, and the end result is stagnation—what you called Japanification.

If inflation or hyperinflation were in our future, then investing in something that the government cannot print could be a good investment, which is what the gold bugs argue for. Gold would remain a precious metal, and its value would remain relatively constant over against a currency being filled up with helium. The currency floats off, and the gold brick stays right there on the ground.

But if the specter that is actually coming at us is the specter of deflation and all-round economic sluggishness, then the gold bug would not lose his shirt because of his gold purchases, but he would lose some value on his hoard. He could have prepared more intelligently for this particular future, but he would probably get through okay.

The real preparation for an uncertain future, according to your take, is investment in human capital. This requires clear vision, a robust eschatology, a biblical anthropology, a grasp of the power of untrammeled markets, and so on. If I had to guess, you would say that a guy in a bunker with a chest full of gold might survive okay, but God put us here to thrive, not simply survive.

The issue is not whether he is putting his resources into the right kind of investment, but rather whether he is becoming the right kind of man.

Is that basically it?

If not, please correct me. If so, then onward to some questions.

If we are talking about the burden of debt, that debt is either strictly unpayable, or we just say it is unpayable in some hyperbolic way, meaning that it could *conceivably* be paid, but only by means of extreme measures. Those extreme measures could include invading another country in order to pillage it, or raising taxes through the roof, which would just be another way of suffocating the economy.

The only other option, it seems to me, is default. If a debt is strictly unpayable, then doesn't that mean it won't ever be paid? And if that is the case, then the only question before the house would be the nature of the default—when will it come, or in what form will it come? My understanding has been that the default would come by means of inflating the currency, paying it off "technically" in a face-saving way, but with the creditor finding that his windfall is now just a bunch of worthless currency.

Another kind of default would be the default *simpliciter*—where the government just says flat out that they are not going to pay it. But I don't think a government could survive something as brazen as that. They at least have to *pretend* to pay, right?

Another tricksy way of defaulting is by "saving Social Security" through "courageous" reforms that change all the rules—like changing the benefits, or the retirement age, and so on. The fact that this kind of thing isn't called a default doesn't keep it from being a default.

This is part of what I had in mind in the distinction between two different kinds of debt. The difference was between reckless overspending now and *promised* reckless overspending down the road. When I have seen the debt burden of the United States discussed, the unfunded liabilities of various entitlement programs are often included. By that I mean things like the promised payouts for Social Security or Medicare ten years from now. That is promised money that doesn't actually exist anywhere yet—like the drunk guy making a bet. When it comes time to pay up, it will then be spent in the way you describe, eating up investment capital that could have been spent more productively. Until that time, there is an opportunity cost in that a person might not be paying into a reliable retirement account because he is relying on the promised government retirement.

So if debt is unpayable, and is steadily increasing, doesn't there *have* to come a moment when the debt is repudiated?

So, on to a few nickel/dime questions.

On your analysis, was the stagflation of the seventies an actual thing? Or was the inflation component of that period an optical illusion?

How would you answer an objection that said that gold and silver prices are being manipulated behind the scenes by various big money players?

If through an odd series of circumstances, you were made the benevolent dictator of a hypothetical country that had crushing debt load, what would you do? What would the way out be? Tax cuts and grow out of it? Regulation cuts and grow out of it? All of the above?

Cordially in Christ,
Douglas

The Fundamental Problem
—BAHNSEN

Dear Douglas,

Allow me to make a few comments on your summary which are intended to be more additive than corrective. It strikes me that a point I made in an earlier letter is useful to revisit when we talk about the "specter of debt" haunting us. I do believe the debt levels, the pay-ability of the debt, and the increasing nature of it all haunt us and carry profound economic implication. But I would be remiss if I did not reaffirm that the fundamental problem, one which trumps the problem of the debt, is the reason for the debt—the size of the government.

The funding and financing schemes behind the size of government are problematic, but they are a symptom of the real problem—that the government is too large, is too much of a part of the gross domestic product of the economy, is too much a part of the societal psychology, and ultimately serves to crowd out the dynamism and productivity of the private sector. This is the heart of the matter. It is not merely the debt that stifles economic growth—that Japanifies us—though that serves a crucial role in the negative feedback loop at play here. Ultimately, if I could pick between a debt-free government that is 50% of the economy, or a deficit-carrying government that is 10% of the economy, I would take the latter every day of the week and twice on Sunday (and I'd have more opportunity to do that twice on Sunday, because the latter is inevitably a more healthy country spiritually).

Moving on to other points of summary you made . . . I am not sure if you are speaking about gold in the context of backing our currency to it, or merely buying it as a pure investment holding. Is the question about gold the wisdom of having a national gold standard (policy) or about holding it as an inflation hedge (personal)? If the latter, it certainly hasn't worked that way in my lifetime, with the price of gold failing to keep up with inflation since I started Kindergarten by about 40%. But I would say that has a lot to do with the moderating inflation rates we have had through much of the last few decades, and gold seemingly better positioned for hyperinflation than moderate-inflation. In other words, the distinction between "inflation" (bad) and "hyperinflation" (really bad) is important when it comes to gold's function, as it may very well help hedge against the latter but not the former.

As for the idea of disinflation or even deflation and its impact on the gold investor, the "losing his shirt" issue comes down to definitions. Gold has compounded at 1.97% per year since I was in Kindergarten, while the stock market has compounded at 9.3% per year. One has basically doubled (gold), while one is up 35x. So no, gold holders have not lost their shirts in this period of disinflation (a lower rate of inflation), but the opportunity cost has been painful.

As to the question of preparation for the future, yes, I would argue that a robust eschatology and biblical anthropology is the need of the hour. Many have been extraordinary investors in human capital and the dynamics of which I speak who lack both, but I would chalk that up as common grace—as the ability to find conclusions with great skill even with incomplete premises. My hope, prayer, and calling is that those who do get the premises fully right will become up to the challenge around the conclusions—that an entrepreneurial investment mentality will come out of our beliefs in human dignity and action; not a bunker mentality, as you mention.

Yes, thriving and not merely surviving.

As for the "pay-ability" of the debt and how exactly this plays out, one thing I have learned loud and clear is that proper and rational humility precludes much specificity in prediction. Underestimating the creativity and optionality of the government in kicking this can is ill-advised. It is true that the legitimate reduction, let alone elimination, of the debt via principal payments strikes me as laughable in any practical sense of math and economics. However, between that and a "default" (failure to make a principal or interest payment) is "perpetual rolling of the debt"—that is, what most developed countries have been doing for decade upon decade—using new debt to retire old debt, all the while servicing the annual cost of the debt.

I am totally fine with the thesis that "this eventually has to stop"—but the burden belongs to that hypothesizer as to when, and what, etc. The idea that "inflating" away the debt is a functional but non-technical default is exactly correct, and it is exactly what the policymakers would do in a heartbeat if they could. Indeed, it is what Japan has been trying to do for the better part of thirty years. My argument is the same as yours—that inflating away debt is a functional but non-technical default, and that it is what policymakers wish they could do (with the appropriate levels of political feasibility and acceptability). But I add to that argument that the very things they do to create these conditions (overly accommodative fiscal and monetary policy) make the outcome more impossible. The debt-disinflation vicious cycle is the buzzsaw they have run into, and has turned their playbook into the equivalent of pushing on a string.

But to the heart of the matter in your question—I do not know if there is a time that the debt has to be repudiated. That moment has not come in the modern era for developed countries, meaning, not in the sense of any technical default. Understand, many could rightly start screaming at me right now that the central bank has bought trillions of dollars of the national debt issuance; that the interest rate levels are being manipulated to keep the debt serviceable; that the currency of other countries playing this same game has been allowed to drop substantially; etc. None of those claims disprove my argument—they make my argument! I did not say it was all clean and above board; I merely said they have ample ways to delay or avoid "technical default" (i.e. repudiation). I now hold their ability to creatively avoid such an outcome (or to at least substantially delay it) in really high regard, and I do not say that as a compliment.

As to some of your other questions . . .

I absolutely see the stagflation of the 1970s as a real thing, which is to say that I see the stagnant economic growth as a real thing, and the monetary inflation of the 1970s as a real thing. If it saves people time to use one word for the two different things that happened, I am all for it. But what ended the stagnation is not up for much debate in the historical record—the pro-growth revolution of the 1980s driven by the supply-side of the economy. There is an important message here.

I wouldn't answer an objection that gold and silver prices are "being manipulated behind the scenes by various big money players." I would merely wait for someone to tell me what the manipulation is, who the players are, how they are doing it, and why they are doing it. Once I had that information I would either learn something new, or have something to reply to. But as a general rule, "behind the scenes manipulation" chatter generally lacks evidence, foundation, and certainly specificity. But it can be fun! One man's manipulation is often another man's open market transaction.

The final question about what direction I would take as a benevolent dictator is a tough one. The hypothetical might mean that I were benevolent dictator of a high debt country whose currency was NOT the world's reserve currency. This changes everything. But I think you are most interested in what I would do if I could wave a wand in this country, right? In specifically

American realities, what would I do? And would you like me to answer in the context of the reality of our social democracy, where political feasibility matters? Or do I have unlimited access to spinach and medicine to impose my will? Let me know how we can box that question in and I will give it a fair shot. I will say that the three principles I would carry to the decision-making process, amongst others, are as follows:

1. There will be no path—none—that is pain-free. Any attempt at resolution that ignores this reality is futile and dishonest *(this will upset many on the left)*.

2. The path ought to be constructed to minimize pain as much as possible. Saying things like, "Sorry if you starve, but your social program must go because we can't afford it"—has some truth in it, and certainly has some red meat for a certain constituency in our society. But it is kind of dumb, kind of heartless, and kind of pointless. I would accept an incremental cure where it mitigated human pain *(this will upset many on the right)*.

3. When you are in a ditch, stop digging. While I would have a lot of work to do to reconcile in a spirit of wisdom #1 and #2, I would not accept

the continued exacerbation of the problem. I would lovingly have to detox the patient, maybe with a little valium for the process, but not with more whiskey.

But with a few more rules of engagement on that final question I will happily dig a bit deeper in our next correspondence!

I hope this is all going in a way you find productive. I appreciate your thoughtful questions and allowing us to wrestle with these things together.

David

Can We Fix the National Deficit?
WILSON

Dear David,

Yes, thank you, and you really are scratching the right itch.

I wasn't so much thinking of gold backing the currency as I was thinking of old Uncle Wyatt, up in his cabin, with a shoebox full of gold coins. And I was not thinking of that question in terms of *investment* wisdom (or lack of it) so much as I was thinking of it as a one-man *insurance* company, buying insurance for himself against the possible horrendous economic prospects to come. In other words, not as a hedge against low-grade inflation, but something more like disaster insurance against runaway train inflation.

If an archangel came down and told absolutely everybody that over the course of the next fifty years, the economy would refuse to do anything drastic—no hyperinflation, no stock market crash, etc.—it seems to me that a bunch of the gold buyers would be more than willing to head on over to the stock market instead. The math behind compound interest can make a pretty compelling case. Your comparison of gold and the stock market was telling.

But the language that these guys use seem to me to be a lot like the language of dedicated clients of insurance companies. Insurance companies have done an enormous amount of research that tells them how likely it is that my house will burn down, and then they offer to bet me a sizable amount of money that they are wrong. So when I buy fire insurance, if I am any good at math, I know that it is in the highest degree likely that a lot more money is going to flow from me to the insurance company than is going to follow from the insurance company to me. That is baked into the whole transaction—but what I am actually buying is peace of mind, and not a way of making money. My insurance payments are not a financial investment, but they are an investment in peace of mind. And peace of mind is what I think these guys are after—and ironically, it doesn't come that way.

Uncle Wyatt has gold under the floorboards because the government can't print it, and he has the idea that there is an inevitable crackup coming—when the government will desperately need to print gold and won't be able to. In other words, I don't think many of them are thinking so much like nine to five steady-as-she-goes investors as they are thinking like someone trying to survive in a mash-up between Thunderdome and the killer bee part of the book of Revelation.

Now if I understand you correctly, that kind of gold bug would be well set if some kind of disastrous hyperinflation hit. Other people would be stuck with worthless paper currency that could just be repudiated, or all the ones and zeros that they had in the bank could just be frozen or seized by the government.

But the reason I brought it up is because I was trying to figure out what gold would do in a deflationary economy. Say that a man could buy a used pick up truck for ten gold coins in 2021, and say he could buy that same truck for $10,000 in Federal Reserve notes. After ten years of hyperinflation, he could buy a comparable truck for ten gold coins, but now it would take $100,000. My numbers are arbitrary—I am not doing any actual math or calculating here. I just want to see what direction all the moving parts are going.

So let us assume that the ten years are not characterized by hyperinflation, but rather by deflation. What does that do to the gold/cash/truck purchase? With inflation, the currency is worth less and less. What happens to the currency in a time of deflation? Does the value of the currency go *up*? Or does it stay the same, but in an economy that is moribund—such that the truck still costs $10,000, but nobody feels like buying it? Because nobody buys trucks in Japan?

Your three-part answer to my question about your benevolent dictatorship actually addressed my question successfully, so no need for more on that.

I am really interested in pursuing further the question of debt over against the size of government. Suppose someone gave me (as they graciously gave you) the choice of living under an administration where the government consumed fifty percent of all the resources, and yet (miraculously) maintained a balanced budget, or I could live under an administration that was continually behindhand, but they were behindhand with a budget that was only ten percent of the nation's economy, like you, I would not even have to think about it. The choice would be between living under a government that suffocated me and a government that routinely embarrassed me.

But don't we have to go by the video, and not by the snapshot? In other words, governments always want to grow their power and influence, and our shared rejection of the first option shows that we value our liberty more than we value a tidy ledger sheet. That really is a slam dunk choice. But isn't it just a snapshot?

If we watch the video of deficit spending in our country, hasn't it usually been an aggrandizing move? I say *usually* instead of *always* because I think there have been a few instances of deficit spending (in wartime, for example) where the government actually retracted to a more reasonable size after the war. But isn't deficit spending a growth hormone that inevitably gets us into bigger and bigger government?

And wouldn't that make our choice of a deficit at ten percent of the economy instead of no deficit at fifty percent like a woman who says she really prefers being two months pregnant over against nine months pregnant?

There are people who have gotten adept at transferring their student loan debt (say) from one 0% credit card to another, and they actually can kick the can down the road. This is to your point about constantly rolling the debt over. But wouldn't this depend on two things remaining constant, both of which are highly unlikely? One is that there would always have to be a credit card company offering 0%—if they quit doing that, then a certain debtor somebody is hosed. And the other is that the person with the debt would have to refrain from adding any more to it.

With regard to the latter, our government has solemnly promised the American people that they won't stop adding to it at ridiculous levels. And with regard to the former, this brings me to my last question. The Fed is currently supplying those 0% credit cards.

Doesn't the current level of the national debt necessitate that the Fed cannot raise interest rates? If they raised rates to "ordinary" levels, wouldn't that cause the national debt to skyrocket into default territory? And as long as they can't raise rates, doesn't that mean that interest rates cannot perform the most valuable function of putting a monetary means of measuring risk? And that means they are stifling the risk-takers and entrepreneurs?

Or is that what you have been maintaining all along? I can be dense . . .

Cordially in Christ,
Douglas

The Stifling of Enterprise
—BAHNSEN

Dear Douglas,

Forgive me for going out of order in my responses here, but there is a little method to my madness.

I want to end up with Uncle Wyatt and his gold under the floorboards because I have a lot to say on him, and I worry if I start with him I will end up waxing and waning too long.

I think a few comments are in order, first, about deficits as a percentage of the economy. You bring up the point that, while we both may agree on the concept that smaller government is better than bigger regardless of deficit spending, the reality is that deficit spending is but a precursor to greater size of government. And I mostly agree, except for the crucial word "inevitably." There is nothing inevitable about it in theory or in practice. In likelihood, I believe so. In current societal attitude, absolutely. But historically, we have had periods where deficits got high, and then collapsed as a percentage of GDP. You brought up the war-time exception, but we really can't look at the biggest example in history as a one-off. The post-WW2 period of shrinking debt-to-GDP lasted for over thirty-five years! That was no blip—it was a generational occurrence, brought on mostly by stellar economic growth through the '50s and '60s.

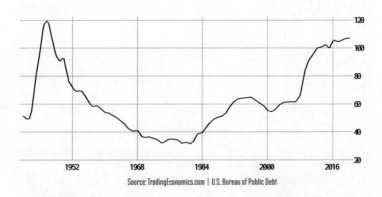

Source: TradingEconomics.com | U.S. Bureau of Public Debt

When we talk about an addicted government spending machine, a look at the contemporary chart would really suggest we are talking about the post-financial crisis era. That is hardly a generational or secular story; it is a societal moment of capitulation to Keynesianism on steroids, devoid of pro-growth policies.

The next visual of this chart (as the post-COVID era makes its way in) will.

But here is the real reason a supply-sider like me has to stand his ground on deficits not being the driver of the problem, but rather overall spending (i.e. size of government)—two things that can correlate, but are not identical. The left would be happy to solve the deficit problem for us—via higher taxes. In fact, they could do it quite easily with a Value-Added tax, a higher marginal tax on the middle class, and then a permission structure to do a candy-bag of tax increases on the wealthy and productive (capital gains, estate, income, corporate, etc.). That would (a) solve the deficit problem, and (b) exacerbate the size-of-government problem ten-fold.

It would be immoral. It would be unfair. It would create stagnation forever and recession for a period. It would crush after-tax wages for the middle class. It would probably lead to populist risings that make recent social unrest look like child's play. It would doom us to permanent sub-trendline growth. But alas, it would eliminate the annual budget deficit!

It's not a trade I would take.

There are pro-growth deficits that I support—Kennedy and Reagan tax cuts on investment that boost supply incentives to the economy. When coupled with a right-sizing of government, those deficits would be

(a) temporary, (b) economically expansionary, and (c) admirable. So because there are scenarios where I believe deficits can be accepted in the overall economic prescription, I have to reiterate my belief that our focus, our priority, our vocabulary, our attention—are all best served by focusing on (a) size of government, which is (b) an inverse to size of self-government in the people, and (c) economic growth and productivity. If we get B and C right, then A will become right, and deficits will be a word in our language that no other word conveniently rhymes with.

I think your point is *practically* true in the modern era—both parties have wanted deficits, and both parties have wanted more government, and those two things have been indistinguishable. My pushback is merely because **it need not be that way,** and because **I believe our focus should be on the big thing, not a frequent symptom of the big thing, and that big thing is inadequate growth and inadequate self-government from the citizenry.**

Now, let me address the issue of bond yields and government debt that you close with, and then come back to Uncle Wyatt—he is okay to wait, I assure you; he doesn't have a lot going on.

Yes, you have found the entire point of what I have been maintaining—that present monetary and fiscal

THE STIFLING OF ENTERPRISE

policy (both) stifle risk-taking and entrepreneurialism, therefore leading to sub-optimal economic growth.

But I do prefer to address some premises you use in getting there. The Fed does not control the interest rate on the debt the government issues. The Fed, in fact, owns barely 20% of the debt the government has issued, the most publicly traded financial security on the globe. They set a target overnight lending rate that depository institutions charge each other (the federal funds rate). They are capable of much manipulation of other rates through various policy measures like quantitative easing (their own buying of bonds). But the world holds U.S. government debt at these brutally low yields—the Fed doesn't make them. Any investor could (and would) sell their bonds because of inadequate yield in a heartbeat (driving yields higher) if they felt the rates were too low (with no participation from the Fed at all). The Fed has been way too interventionist in all of this—from the zero percent overnight lending rate, to buying trillions of dollars of government debt over the last thirteen years with a computer screen. But the specific issue of the government's cost of borrowing is set by the market, even with interventions and distortions as they are. The vast majority of our debt is held by investors and by foreign countries who need dollars.

I simply want to get the criticism right, and the fact pattern right. The Fed distorts. It seeks to impose prices

instead of allowing for the discovery of prices. It creates moral hazard in financial markets by coddling asset
holders. And most of all, its easy monetary policy allows
"zombie" companies to survive—companies who can
keep the lights on because the low rate environment
creates a financial survival that would otherwise lead to
creative destruction. This means poorly allocated capital stays poorly allocated, whereas it could otherwise
be funding new projects, companies, technologies, and
innovations that are more productive and opportunis-
tic. This is the essence of the Fed's distortion in markets, and I have nothing good to say about it.

But the U.S. government has a low cost of debt for
plenty of reasons besides the Fed. For one thing, European and Japanese debt is at an even lower cost. In other words, global investors need our debt because it is
positively profitable compared to the negative carry
they get with other developed alternatives. But more
important than anything else, the U.S. dollar is the
world's reserve currency. Our current account deficit
is settled in our own currency. We are the largest trading partner in the world (we buy a lot more than we
sell), and as a country we are terrible at saving. Therefore, we need the world to fund our deficits which they
are happy to do because "there is no alternative." Will
Chinese renminbi one day replace the U.S. dollar in
this capacity? Well, I wouldn't bet on it, but that would

be one theory, I suppose. Will the Euro? That sounds laughable. The Yen? More laughable.

This is a sadder part of the story. As you and I analyze our country's negligence in fiscal sanity and responsibility, we would actually have to give the U.S. a better grade if we graded on a curve, based on the even worse record of competitive nations. Now, that is changing. The post-COVID maneuvers of our leaders (with the full support of the people) have us playing fast catchup. But my point is that one has to be able to envision a time when the dollar loses currency reserve status, and to do that one has to have the imagination to guess what will replace it. You can see why those roulette odds in predicting all this (let alone adding a timetable to it) keep diminishing.

I would suggest two other considerations are in order when we try to think about how this all ends. One is the lesson of Japan. We went from being "really irresponsible fiscally" to "grotesquely irresponsible" about eighteen months ago. They have been "perversely irresponsible and then some" for thirty years. What have the consequences been? No default. No spike in interest rates. No inflation whatsoever. No great depression. A generation of deflation and disinflation? Yes. Absolutely no economic growth? Yes. A currency that is the envy of no one? Sure. But any predictions one would have, perhaps sensibly, offered around how their story would go would have been profoundly wrong, for an inordinate amount of time.

Now, they owe most of their debt to themselves. They do not require, need, or even want many foreign buyers of debt. They do not need to fund a military. I merely want to point out how dangerous the prediction business is here with the United States. We have a million things going for us *better* than Japan does (for now), and they have been unable to reach the point of reconstructionist-version Armageddon for decades.

This is the furthest thing from a sanguine view of Japan's predicament, let alone ours. It is simply an empirical basis for not believing that we can see how (or when) this fiscal mess in the United States will play out. The part I can see, though, is exactly what you conclude with: **the stifling of risk-taking and entrepreneurs.** This is my great priority.

And this brings me back to Uncle Wyatt. There are a number of self-refuting assumptions in that predicament you describe I want to highlight. In your scenario, Uncle Wyatt merely has "insurance" under his floorboards. It is "sleep at night" money. He believes for some bizarre reason that the government will one day need to "print gold" and because it can't there would be chaos—Thunderdome, revelation, Y2K type stuff. I get it.

But why can't the government change conversion rates of gold (they already did)? Why can't the government confiscate the gold (they already did)? Why can't they eliminate its role as a medium of exchange (they already did)? In fact, they did some of this well before they ever took away the gold standard. In other words, the fundamental thesis of the gold bugs (an underground currency to protect against government abuse) is undermined by, well, a government that can abuse. Gold is immune from such scenarios? Not in history; not in theory; not in reality. Gold owners are safe from such? I would argue they are more exposed.

So if Uncle Wyatt sleeps better with the small risk of theft, small risk of weather erosion or natural disaster, and small risk of price depreciation, up against whatever risk it is he is more concerned about, I wouldn't stop him. I want Uncle Wyatt to get his rest. But on a risk/ reward basis, can we at least see how incredibly dumb this trade-off has been, and continues to be? If we end up with the worst case scenario Uncle Wyatt is envisioning, who exactly does he think is going to be his counter party? Who will he buy his flat screen TV from? How will he get to the Mexican Riviera for vacation?

Now, maybe he just wants to stay in his cabin and be ready to shoot any stormtroopers that come his way. Fair enough. But now we get close to me being able to make my point—this is not an economic position; it is

a sociological one. I freely admit it is not my sociology;
I just wish Uncle Wyatt would admit it is his.

I believe gold has been a hedge in times of hyperinflation in the past, but I am not sure how it would do
if America suffered hyperinflation. The reach of our
government and the statism that would follow economic collapse would likely alter expectations a great
deal. In Third-World countries gold has performed
that function, but the very thing gold bugs are worried about (statist overreach) changes the reality in the
States, in my view.

In a period of real deflation, cash is worth more and
assets are worth less. Disinflation is a more likely scenario, and it means a price level not shrinking but growing
at a shrinking rate. That is the world we have been living
in as the national debt has gone from sub-$10 trillion to
soon $30 trillion. Great efforts are being extended to
create higher inflation to break this negative feedback
loop and allow for debt retirement with inflated dollars,
and all those efforts (fiscal and monetary kitchen sinks)
are resulting in, well, more stagnation.

I would not wish ill on Uncle Wyatt if he could hear
my whole argument, understand a little better than he
likely does the vocabulary of the terms he uses, and
yet in the end, just feels better with gold coins in his
basement. Most of the Uncle Wyatts I have known
have been nice guys, even if I probably wouldn't drop

my kids off for an extended stay. But in aspiring for an optimal economic worldview, one cannot help but notice that there is a parable of the talents deficiency with that thinking.

I want Uncle Wyatt to sell his gold coins for the same reason I want Uncle Sam to quit spending so much money. Because when both things happen, the cause of human flourishing is advanced.

David

Who's Afraid of Stagnation?

—WILSON

Dear David,

This discussion has been most helpful.

I found your reference to the parable of the talents striking, and more than a little bit on the nose. In that parable, the "wicked servant" is the one who is risk averse. He is a take-no-chances sort of follow (Matt. 25:25), perhaps a distant ancestor of our Uncle Wyatt. The other two servants were given five and two talents respectively, and they took what they had been given and went out and did something risky with them.

Another way of putting this is that the parable *could* have had a different financial result, but with the same spiritual evaluation being applied to the servants. The servant with five talents could have lost his shirt along with everything else. The servant with two talents might have had the ship that was carrying his investment back sink in a storm. And the servant who buried the one talent might have been the only one of the three who returned anything of financial worth to his master. But he *still* would have been the wicked servant. Whatever happened with the money, the whole operation was having an effect on the men. It seems that budgeting for the possibility of failure is something that two of them did, and one of them did not want to do, and his failure was that he could not see the possible blessing associated with something like that.

The master was entrusting a lot to them, and the servants who risked it were risking a lot. A talent was about seventy-five pounds, and at the time of my writing the spot price of silver is around $25 per ounce and gold around $1,835. If we are talking silver, that's around $30K for the guy with one talent, and if gold, then $2.2M. And while they were investing their master's money in various projects, the master was actually investing in *them*. And out of three investments, the master had a good return on two of them.

So if I am tracking with you, your problem with Uncle Wyatt is not that he is protecting himself, but rather that he is not guarding himself against the real risk—the risk of becoming the kind of risk-averse person who basically paralyzes himself. The wicked lazy servant set out to protect himself in the first instance, and the one thing he did not successfully do was protect himself.

You say that his strategy is actually making him *more* vulnerable, more exposed. Are you saying this because one of the first things that would happen in some sepia-toned apocalypse is that somebody in the mob is going to shout, "Hey, I know where the preppers live!"? And then someone else chimes in with information about where all the Mormon food is.

So the issue is not really the money. The issue is what kind of person the investor is becoming. A risk averse person can easily think that it is also about the money, when it is actually all about *him*. A related issue is what kind of communities then grow up around such inventors, investors, and entrepreneurs. If we have another thousand years of economic growth and development before us, then we are squandering a lot right now if we turn into an economic version of dispensational pre-millennialists. Would you think it a fair assessment if we were to say that one of the problems with the hard money recons is that they never worked their postmillennialism into their economic views?

I am tracking with your larger argument here, and am in hearty agreement with it. But I still have a few practical questions. I agree that if given a choice

between large government/no deficit and small government/manageable deficit, we should take the latter.
You outline a situation where the government swells
up because of the heavy taxes they lay on us, and then
say that, on the other hand, "It would eliminate the
annual budget deficit!"

But wouldn't it be better to say that it *could* eliminate
the deficit? What would prevent a government, hungry
to grow, from piling on the heavy taxes *and also* going
in for huge deficits? It seems to me that we should want
to cultivate an instinctive loathing for both big government and big deficits. I say this while taking your
point that you want to do this as well, but that you are
having trouble articulating a scary enough catastrophe
that would help the average guy get his mind around it.
Everybody understands how bad an economic F5 tornado would be, a la Larry Burkett, but nobody would
take any drastic measures to prepare in advance for two
decades of economic sluggishness. Nobody is going to
run for the hills to get away from Japanification. They
went to Japan once, when they were in the navy, and it
seemed like an ordinary place. Is this a fair statement of
the challenge you have when it comes to communicating your position to conservatives?

It is not that I think we should invent something
scary in order to get good outcomes. But is there an

effective way to describe just how bad our irresponsibility is going to make life for our great-grandchildren?

You also say:

"I believe our focus should be on the big thing, not a frequent symptom of the big thing, and that big thing is inadequate growth and inadequate self-government from the citizenry."

I agree with this also, and so it would seem we have to agree that another downside of large government is not just the oxygen they take away from our rooms of business, in the form of taxes, but also the poison gas they pump into those same rooms, in the form of onerous regulations. What would happen if the tax burden were cut in half, and the regulatory burden were also? Or would you say that all we need to do is cut taxes because that is where the salaries of the regulators come from?

One last thing. You brought up (in passing) something that I hoped we would get to somehow, and that is the question of trade deficits. You said, "We are the largest trading partner in the world (we buy a lot more than we sell) . . ." and you said this with a cheerful tone in your voice. I have felt (for many years) that there was something seriously off in the standard trade deficit concerns. When it comes to household economics, I have never worried about more coming in than going out, and I wonder if you could help me out here. And does this question relate in any way to the broader concerns we have been discussing?

Cordially in Christ,
Douglas

The Problem of Risk Aversion
—BAHNSEN

Dear Douglas,

I think your exegesis and extended commentary on the parable of the talents is really quite spectacular, and I do believe you have captured much of my beliefs on the subject. I think that the "risk averse" person who matches our caricature known as Uncle Wyatt has failed in a few ways. For our purposes, the most significant one is the one you have highlighted—that there is a lack of understanding in Uncle Wyatt's thinking (what I often erroneously or otherwise refer to as the sociology behind it) regarding what wealth is, and where it comes from. You mentioned in prior correspondence

holding George Gilder in high regard, and one thing
his work has profoundly taught me is understanding
wealth as the growth of goods and services that comes
from knowledge, ideas, and risk. I believe a country can
have more units of capital (whether it be that nation's
currency or gold bars or what have you) than a competitive country, but less wealth, in that what defines
the prosperity of a nation (or a family, or a community,
etc.) will always be the sum total of "supply" (i.e. goods
and services that actionably create quality of life). Uncle
Wyatt is not investing in wealth creation.

Now, the financial advisor in me wants to point out a
few other things about "risk aversion" besides the spiritual and textual points you have helped extract. I still
believe many "gold bugs" believe that "well, I may be
missing out on the great returns of the stock market,
but at least I avoid volatility and the risk of price depreciation while the government goes about their business
of acting insane." We have spent plenty of time talking
about the realities and misunderstandings of inflation,
and what actually has and has not outpaced inflation
over meaningful periods of time. But from a pure "risk
aversion" standpoint, it is important to note that gold
was at $1,800 in 2012, and spent most of 2013–2018
around $1,200, a 33% drop that lasted many years,
despite all the governmental and monetary insanity of
the last decade. Gold was at $800 in 1980, and was at

$250 in 2001, a 75% drop over a two-decade period. Now, it has had big runs up and big runs down along the way, and maybe Uncle Wyatt didn't care about multi-year and multi-decade declines in price, but I do believe it undermines the idea of "risk aversion." I would suggest those that "ride out" such price volatility actually have more risk aversion capacity than they have told themselves.

So to summarize, I believe that the mentality of those who bypass wealth-creating investments for the risk aversion of "survivalist" strategies like gold are (a) failing to invest in wealth creation, and (b) failing to invest in risk aversion.

Your question about whether or not hard money recons have worked their eschatology into their economic views is an astute one. In a lot of ways I think one of the reasons I shunned the hard money "sociology" of the free market postmillennial friends I largely grew up around is because I became too free market and too postmillennial for it. I recognize many of them state that they do believe in the eventual success of markets, enterprise, and of course, gospel transformation, but first believe we have to be eating each other in the wilderness before society can change. And maybe that will happen. But theologically, I have never found the argument compelling that a societal collapse has to or will happen before gospel transformation can

commence. And I have certainly not found it historically compelling that an economic collapse will see to
it that wealth-creating investments all die while "under
the mattress" investments thrive. It strikes me as not
only historically unsubstantiated, but ideologically
counterintuitive.

On to some of your practical questions . . . I am in
wholehearted agreement that the ideal scenario is one
of small government and one that lacks big deficits.
Small, temporary deficits that come from seasonal or
cyclical revenue volatility do not bother me, and temporary deficits that come in the "Laffer's curve" process of reducing marginal tax burden certainly do not
bother me. However, I freely recognize that is not what
we have created. Large and structural and intentionally
permanent deficits are the status quo, and I reject them
as policy prescriptions out of hand.

So to your question of how we communicate the
scariness of Japanification—of long-term economic
stagnation—I believe we have two things in front of us
that will really move the needle.

We have to regain economic credibility by imple-
menting a cease and desist on false prophecy. If the
"hard money recon" club decided to rebrand around
the fears of Japanification tomorrow, they would have
a hard time getting an audience (for one thing, their
audience likes the message of economic catastrophe,

but for another, the years of credibility damage are significant). There is work to do here to regain a listening audience in this field. But I promise you, I am working on it daily!

We can tell the story vividly and frequently of a society that fails to achieve trendline economic growth. It's almost like we could point to populist uprisings that come about when whole classes of people fail to see historical growth achieved. Heck, we could even threaten them with a British exit from the European Union and a Donald Trump presidency if we have to! But in all seriousness, the wage stagnation story is profound. The housing unaffordability story is compelling. And a few charts and figures could be assembled that illustrate how significant the Japanese quality of life has suffered from 2–3 decades of stagnation. But, at the end of the day, I would prefer taking a more positive approach. The negativity of long term Japanification may lack sex appeal, but the positivity of wealth creation is inspiring. I believe we need to sell it on the basis of opportunity cost. We need to present a full capacity enterprise economy to the church. That vision is the inverse of what we are selling now, and it is the other side to the same coin. I think it is more motivating.

I love your question about tax cuts vs. deregulation. I do not believe merely cutting taxes will be sufficient. Deregulation is a better way to get to tax cuts than tax cuts are a way to getting to deregulation. The size of the administrative state is the cause du jour of the central planner, and it is public enemy number one for the risk-taker. Regulation is not merely a path to a more complex and insidious state, but it is the path to creation of monopolistic mediocrities in business that use regulation as a subsidy—to crowd out real organic competition. With regulation comes cronyism, always and forever. The supply-side war is one of incentives, and nothing incentivizes productivity more than deregulation.

Finally, on trade deficits, I appreciate you bringing this issue up. I continue to run a pretty substantial trade deficit with the gal in New York City who does my hair. The only thing I have ever given her is money, and the only thing she gives me is a haircut. I have become comfortable with this economic relationship, and that ongoing trade deficit remains (I bring no goods or services to the table with her; just cash). You ask what this subject may have to do with our other topics, and I would propose two things that should not be taken lightly:

The use of the word "deficit" in the phrase "trade deficit" has sufficiently poisoned the well to create an aura of negativity that is economically fallacious, but rhetorically effective.

Those who bemoan our trade deficit with China, for example, fail to understand how the low savings rate of the United States and the high budget deficit of the United States screamed for a high trade deficit. In other words, while the general understanding of the matter is that China got dollars and international credibility from being a big exporter of goods to the U.S., and the U.S. got cheap stuff at Walmart from China, the fact of the matter is that the biggest advantage to the United States was not cheap stuff. We paid China for their exports in dollars, and they then turned around and bought treasuries with the dollars we gave them. Our deficit was their surplus—and that reinvestment of the dollars we gave them back into the United States was a pivotal part of U.S. deficit funding over the last twenty-five years. China's foreign exchange reserves make up for the U.S.'s low savings rate. This element of the mutually convenient economic arrangement has not gotten a lot of press (let's just say I don't believe the prior president had a firm grasp on this), and it is an important part of the conversation.

All current accounts are zero when it comes to international trade. We may import ten, export eight, and pay out cash of two, but the ledgers equal out in the end. To the extent there is inequity, it is likely in how the participants are able to use the value of their currency to game those equations, not in leaving unpaid debt on the ledgers. And since we hold the world's reserve currency, and we get to settle our current account deficits with our own currency, well, I would say we have held a large advantage there.

None of this addresses human rights issues, or technology protections, or national security, or an optimal domestic manufacturing policy, etc. But as for the mere trade deficit of it all, I will come back to the prior definition of wealth I offered. I believe "total trade" (exports + imports) is what matters—not the "trade deficit" (exports – imports). The trade deficit collapses in a recession, yet no one seems happy about it. Some of the most impoverished nations on earth run trade surpluses. The total activity in an economy and the law of comparative advantage all speak to "total trade" as a better indication of national prosperity.

So whether we are talking about trade deficits or budget deficits, I remain firmly committed to the idea of high enterprise, low government, and a Church that is ready for the demands of both.

David

What Kind of Men Should We Be?

—WILSON

Dear David,

I need to thank you very much for these exchanges. They have been very helpful to me, and I hope they will be the same for others.

Before I summarize how I think we have covered the waterfront, and ask a few final questions related to that, I do have to ask a very pertinent question first. In the time it has taken us to write these exchanges, the prices of more than a few commodities have been behaving in such a way as might make numerous conservatives want to reject your thesis. A lot of prices have gone up, everybody appears to understand that inflation is a really bad thing (and they know what it is, more or less), and conservatives see a golden opportunity to hang this particular inflation bubble around Joe Biden's neck.

In other words, however inconvenient the timing may be for you and me in trying to persuade conservative America that the real threat is deflation, nevertheless the timing remains very convenient to hammer Biden with. And so that leads to the question I *have* to ask you as we wrap up. While we have been writing this book, a lot of conservative pundits have announced to the world that inflation really has taken off. I have seen charts and everything. Has anything happened in the last twelve months to make you reconsider?

In other words, is there *any* chance that we might publish this book, and within about three months, say, Canon Press might be forced to raise the price of it to $300? And there you and I will be, doubly damned as inflation deniers. In other words, are you sure about all this? Is the bond market still doing the same thing it was when we started writing?

Okay. With that out of the way, let me attempt to summarize your take on inflation. It is not that you believe that our current handlers are too virtuous to inflate the currency, because you believe they would absolutely do it if they could just figure out how. The soil is saturated with water, and as much as it might benefit them if the soil were to absorb some more, it is just not going to.

If we define inflation as extra currency pursuing the same amount of goods, there are two components to this. One is the creation of that extra currency, and the other is the task of getting that currency actually to *pursue* those goods. In other words, we have to factor in both the *amount* of currency and the *velocity* of the currency. If the government printed a boatload of new money, but did not put it into circulation, there would be no inflation. If the government printed a boatload of new money, put it into circulation, and then the banks and the borrowers then said something like *meh*, the effect would be minimal inflation. In order for inflation to really take off, the currency has to be willing to do some chasing.

But this way of expressing it hides something, and maybe it is something crucial. Perhaps this way of expressing things is the source of much of our confusion. Currency doesn't chase anything, people with currency chase things. Gold doesn't horde itself, people with gold horde it. Printing presses don't expand the currency, officials at the Fed make their decisions to expand the currency, and then go home to dinner. In other words, monetary policy, and the economic consequences of monetary policy, *are personal*. And when all these people are making their respective decisions, they are doing so out of the framework of a particular worldview.

And this brings me back to our poor Uncle Wyatt. He is concerned about whether his purchasing power is going to be devalued by runaway inflation. That is his focus. And if I take you right, your emphasis is that you don't want Uncle Wyatt himself to be devalued. He is the actual resource, and *he* is the thing that must not be squandered, frittered away, or buried in a napkin in the ground.

Money doesn't do things. People do things. As von Mises has it in his title, economics is all about *human action*. Money simply measures the things that people do, and if we are going to be jealous about any resource, the thing we should be most jealous about is the greatest resource—which is the people who take risks. And this is why we should want to preach the kind of hot gospel that creates the kind of people who take those risks. The way we sometimes talk, it is as though we think the yard markers on the sidelines of the football game are capable of making first downs.

And in a free economy, people don't take risks (for the most part) because they are daredevils. They take risks because of who and what they love. Civilizations are built by men who have families to feed.

And this means that no currency was ever corrupted unless the worldview of the people is corrupted first.

No talent was ever buried in the ground unless the faithless steward entrusted with it was buried in the ground first. In other words, all the disasters of monetary policy we might be able to itemize, and there have been many, they all have a counterpart in the hearts of the people. And that is where the real trouble is.

Put another way, it would be better to be the kind of man who took risks in order to build, invest, and provide—in other words, to love—than to be the kind of man who hesitated with regard to everything because he was tangled up in fear and insecurity. Even if he turned out to be right about the gold, he would have been wrong about *himself*, which means that he wouldn't be any good managing his store of gold through the zombie apocalypse. A lifetime of risk aversion would be no help at all during a zombie apocalypse, or so it would seem. And another man who—again for the sake of love—had thrown himself into the exigencies of life for the sake of his people, may have "lost money" as he did it, but he would be the kind of man you would want to have by your side while shotgunning zombies. Again, so to speak.

In sum, Scripture tells us that in our day-to-day lives, we interact with two things that are forever, and our financial portfolio is not one of them.

"Lay not up for yourselves treasures upon earth, where moth and rust doth corrupt, and where thieves

break through and steal: But lay up for yourselves treasures in heaven, where neither moth nor rust doth
corrupt, and where thieves do not break through nor
steal" (Matthew 6:19–20).

The first thing we deal with every day that is forever
is the Word of God:

"The grass withereth, the flower fadeth: But the
word of our God shall stand for ever" (Isaiah 40:8).

And the second thing would be the people we are
surrounded by, whether Christians or not.

"And have hope toward God, which they themselves
also allow, that there shall be a resurrection of the dead,
both of the just and unjust" (Acts 24:15).

And that, naturally, is where our long term investments should be.

"And I say unto you, make to yourselves friends of
the mammon of unrighteousness; that, when ye fail,
they may receive you into everlasting habitations"
(Luke 16:9).

> Cordially in Christ,
> Douglas

Our Government and Self-Government

—BAHNSEN

Dear Douglas,

I, too, have enjoyed the exchanges, and share your hope that they will be for others.

I appreciate the opportunity to launch this final round of correspondence with one final reiteration and affirmation in the light of current events. You are absolutely correct that many see present price escalations as a chance to score political points against President Biden, and no one can really blame them. One of the most non-partisan realities of American political life is that whoever is in office when X happens will be blamed for X. It is sometimes true, sometimes not true at all, and often times a little bit true. The Democrats would do the same if a Republican were in office now. And we have ample historical precedent for this basic political fact—those in office get the blame for what is happening when they are in office.

But the question is not what the political opportunity is here, an issue that I fully expect to play out to the Republican advantage for the time being. The question is whether or not *government spending in the current moment is the cause of current price escalations.* That is correlated to the question of whether or not government spending is inherently inflationary. My answer is, "Yes, and then no." It can have an inflationary impact before it gets exposed to the law of diminishing returns. We have corresponded at length on that subject. But in the present moment are the price escalations we see the sudden consequence of President Biden's excessive spending? Are the present escalations the sudden consequence of the Fed's accommodative monetary policies? To answer "yes" would invite the burden of explaining why the trillions of dollars of excessive government spending under a Republican predecessor were *not* inflationary, but the excessive spending of a Democrat replacement was. Why were Fed policies (of unprecedented accommodation) from 2008–2020 (that is a long time) *not* inflationary, but in 2021, they suddenly were?

Well, all chance for political point-scoring to the side (something I have already said I accept as a part of political reality), the response that "Republican over-spending is non-inflationary while Democrat over-spending is inflationary" is not going to cut the mustard. And perhaps even less cogent would be the statement that "Fed policy transitions from non-inflationary to inflationary when the White House changes uniforms, even when the people and policies of the Fed do not." You get my point.

So this leads me to the deduction that there are price escalations taking place in the economy, and that the causation may be different than what was previously *not* causing such. Now, one could propose that the potential catalysts merely had a delayed response, but that lacks evidence, and faces the brutal counterfactual of Japan. And such convenient theorizing is not necessary when we have such superior explanations on the page. Allow me to move from Economics class to Algebra for a moment.

Irving Fisher's Quantity Theory of Money states that $MV=PT$. That is, the Money Supply (M) multiplied by the Velocity of money (V) will be equal to the Price Level (P) multiplied by the Total Supply of Goods and Services (T). It is a fundamental equation, and can be re-stated as $P=MV/T$. In other words, the price level is equal to the Money Supply multiplied by Velocity, divided by Total Supply. We focus often on

Milton Friedman's idiom that inflation is "too much money chasing too few goods," and see the M (Money supply) as the key ingredient ("inflation is always and everywhere a monetary phenomenon"). For the last couple decades the stable velocity that Milton got to take for granted fought against the monetarist idea of rising money supply as inherently inflationary. Declining velocity offset rising money supply, and as you know from our correspondence, I see that declining velocity as the key ingredient many inflationistas so badly missed. I further see that declining velocity as the result of the economic stagnation that excessive fiscal and monetary activity create.

But now, we not only have a rising M being offset by a declining V, but we do have a declining T causing the P to necessarily rise. Taking out the identity code, we have a rising money supply against a declining velocity, mostly rendering each other useless in explanation for price levels increasing, with the supply of goods and services being the key ingredient. And this suffering supply exists in a moment when demand is flying through the roof post-COVID. Somehow, politicians who locked down the economy for what seemed like forever are shocked that newly liberated prisoners want to go out to dinner. Go figure.

Politicians are practically paid to get this stuff wrong, but we must be better. We do not have price escalations because all of a sudden after infinite examples to the contrary the Fed buying bonds from banks proved inflationary. We have price escalations because the gap between demand and supply has accelerated behind growing demand and a perfect storm of supply inadequacy. Supply inadequacy? Poor investment in semiconductor manufacturing. A total collapse of labor participation. Union silliness hurting port capacity. A huge shortage of truck drivers. A huge shortage of truck driver applicants that can pass a drug test. A shutdown of rigs and timber mills just in time for the demand for oil and gas and lumber to accelerate. A real perfect storm of cultural, political, and economic forces that have constrained supply into a period of "pent up" demand.

I should say that I do not believe all of these elements are apolitical. If the goal for some is to find political blame for price escalations, one can find political culprits sprinkled throughout, but it isn't the clean hit that "government spending did it!" is. And I should say, the various incentives, transfer payments, and societal coddling that has helped to structurally limit 19 to 25-year-olds in the workforce and 55+-year-olds in the workforce have been highly prevalent throughout the last year of the prior administration into the first year of the new administration. It is still riddled with political fingerprints, but there are the fingerprints of two parties on it, so that's no fun.

But you ask the key question here that answers how structural these price escalations are, and how monetary they are in their causation—"is the bond market still doing the same thing it was when we started writing?" As I type this email, the yield on a ten-year Treasury bond is 1.50%. When we started the correspondence it was 1.50%. It has hit 1.80% and it has hit 1.20% over this last year, but the bond market has continued to view price level growth as inherently non-sustainable. I make it a habit of not fighting the bond market for the same reason I do not argue with my wife—I am not going to win, ever.

So moving on from the current moment, I want to reiterate that the best word to capture what I am now expecting is "stagnation"—not inflation, and not really even deflation. Unfortunately, "deflationary" pressures take hold during real recessions, but even in non-recessionary and non-contractionary periods, we are pushing on a string in trying to get economic growth, let alone in trying to get the inflation that you rightly surmise I believe the current handlers want. I expect more disinflation than deflation (i.e. a declining rate of growth of inflation), but the natural order of things all this fiscal and monetary mess has created is deflationary, and central bankers live on planet Earth to fight deflation, no matter what they say when the microphone is on.

Your summary of how a real economy is measured, how a real economy grows, and what true economic anthropology looks like, is simply beautiful. My advocacy is for risk-taking, not rent-seeking; for humanity, not government; for a sanctified citizenry, not merely a stable currency. I think you get an inverse correlation with some of these things naturally, but the catalyst and driver to productive economic results must be the faithful obedience of the human person living in their natural design for productivity that mirrors the image of the God who made them.

Earnest conversations exist about various aspects of governmental policies and distortions, and more in the weeds, about the subject of currency debasement and general price inflation. But I am convinced as you summarize that we have too much government creating too much economic stagnation because we have too little self-government creating too little productivity. My economic burden is for a morally enlightened citizenry to be faithful in their mandate to grow and steward creation. And this is where the inflation/deflation debate can end in obsoletion:

*Where humans are acting in faithful obedience to God's design for us as creative risk-takers and producers, we crush the inflation of too much money chasing too few goods, **and** the deflation of economic stagnation.*

David

Appendix

—BAHNSEN

Some interesting things have continued to unfold in the economy since Pastor Wilson and I first began our correspondence. The Consumer Price Index in early 2022 sits 7% higher than it was in 2021. Home prices have reached parabolic levels. And inflation is wrapped around the neck of President Biden as perhaps the most significant political liability he and the Democratic Party face going ino a midterm election year.

The particulars when discussing inflation matter. One of the points I make in the correspondence with Pastor Wilson is that an "aggregate price level" doesn't exist. Inflation does not effect all goods and services at all times in the same way. The reason should be obvious—the particular circumstances that impact prices are vast, complex, filled with variables, and therefore are not level across all goods and services. Therefore, to weight these things together into a single aggregate is unhelpful. The analogy I used was "national weather"—it is unhelpful to the golfer in Wisconsin and the golfer in Florida to know what "average weather conditions" are across the United States.

I believe we have lived with above-acceptable inflation in three areas for a whole generation: Housing prices, college tuition, and health care costs. And as it turns out, these three areas all share one thing in common that establish indisputable proof, not post hoc fallacy, of the cause of that price inflation: Government subsidy. The government's inexcusable interventions in subsidizing capital to the home market through the multi-trillion dollar entities that are Fannie Mae and Freddie Mac, not to mention the government's monopolistic intrusion in the student loan market, have given a carte blanche structure for price increases. Distorting the cost of capital and access to capital has pushed prices higher in housing, as any first-year economics student could have predicted.

But worse, most people think that is a wonderful thing! When is the last time you heard a homeowner complain about their high home price value?

Milton Friedman was right: People hate inflation, until they don't.

Government subsidies in these three massive areas of the economy have created a structural inflation that is largely isolated to those three areas. But what about the cyclical inflation of 2021? Do we now face 5-8% inflation rates in food and cars because of 2021 government spending and Fed monetary policy?

I try to be as non-partisan as possible as an economist, believing that my policy views should flow from my economic philosophy, not that my economic philosophy should flow from my political views. I am not totally sure how to interpret those who believe trillions of dollars of government spending (including direct payments to taxpayers) in a Republican administration is not inflationary, but it becomes such when it is a Democrat administration. What the Biden spending bill of 2021 was is this: Excessive, reckless, irresponsible, unnecessary, unaffordable, and wrong. And, short-term, it surely increased consumer spending.

But alas, like all excesses that have to be purged, the hangover hurts more than the bender felt good. And ultimately, government spending has proven time and time again to add to the velocity problem I talk about in this book. The money in circulation ends up dormant, and loan demand collapses because there are less borrow-worthy projects and less borrow-worthy borrowers. Rinse and repeat.

The nuances of current price inflation, cyclical as they are, require the admission of different variables in the mix: Declining Chinese production capacity in COVID, U.S. energy rigs being taken off-line and then facing an anti-fossil radicalism in the White House, a tragic resignation of U.S workers, a collapse of semiconductor manufacturing (perhaps the largest factor in this list), and of course, well-documented challenges at U.S. ports and with U.S. truckdrivers. If the Fed raised interest rates to 10% tomorrow (Volcker style), it would not put a single truckdriver back on duty. This is a wild set of circumstances that has driven prices higher in a cyclical context.

But the current narrative, as politically beneficial as I totally understand it to be for those of us on the right, still does not negate these facts:

1. Housing prices, college tuition, and health care costs face structural inflation because of government subsidy, and that is both wrong and correctable. It will not be corrected because the people like their home price inflation, and they like unlimited capital for student debt.

2. The current price inflation will reverse when aforementioned cyclical circumstances reverse. But the debt levels taken on will not. And that debt is deflationary to the extreme, suffocating

future growth in the most classic sense possible.
See: Japan.

3. Our economic ailment is a matter of inadequate
   growth. In cyclical inflation a growth of output
   solves all—more goods and services soaking up
   more money supply. In structural stagnation/
   disinflation, more growth reverses the stagnation
   and produces the environment for humans acting (the definition of economics). Humans act
   rationally because God made them with reason.
   And it is irrational to invest in robust growth
   when excessive indebtedness is suffocating future
   growth opportunity.

As Pastor Wilson and I have gone to great lengths to
lay out in this book, the solution is an economic theology of growth. Savings = Investments (a tautology,
since a dollar invested has to first be a dollar saved).
More savings equals more investment and more investment equals more productivity and more productivity
equals more growth. Therefore, more savings equals
more growth. Excessive debt means less savings. And
that means, less growth.

A country that spends within its means can grow.
And that is the moral need of the hour—growth.

An economic theology of growth is not the moral
need of the hour merely because used car prices have

gone too high in 2022. It is the moral need of the hour because of the Garden of Eden. To that end, I work.

David

DAVID BAHNSEN'S
DIVIDEND CAFE
VIDEO BLOG

DOUG WILSON'S
BLOG & MABLOG
VIDEO SERIES

WATCH WEEKLY ON CANON+

MYCANONPLUS.COM

There's No Free Lunch

BY DAVID BAHNSEN

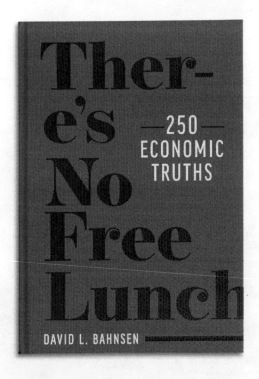

"David's book mixes the old and the new, the classical and the modern, and does so in a readable way that teaches readers what they need to know about economics. No matter what you've been taught, or what you think you believe, your understanding of economics will benefit and expand by reading this superb book."

—LARRY KUDLOW

NOFREELUNCHECONOMICS.COM

DOUG WILSON

Ploductivity

*A Practical
Theology of Work*

CANONPRESS.COM

Ploductivity: n, 1) the practice of plodding away at a pile of work, instead of frantically trying to sprint through it all

2) being stable and graceful, like a buffalo upon the plains, not frantic, like a prairie dog or roadrunner